HUNGRy
FOR
MORE
OF

JESUS

"I know of one sure place where the supply of Bread never fails, and that is the secret closet of prayer. The Holy Spirit waits there to bring this precious Bread to you, to satisfy you completely, and to make you strong and able to resist the world and the devil. If you are hungry for more of Jesus, then come to the Lord's table often. Be diligent to keep the feast. There you will find the abundant life He longs to give you."

from ***Hungry for More of Jesus***

HUNGRY FOR MORE OF

JESUS

DAVID WILKERSON

Chosen Books

A Division of Baker Book House Co
Grand Rapids, Michigan 49516

Unless noted otherwise Scripture quotations are from
The New King James Version. Copyright © 1979,
1980, 1982 Thomas Nelson, Inc., Publishers.

Scripture quotations identified NASB are from the New
American Standard Bible, copyright © The Lockman
Foundation 1960, 1962, 1963, 1968, 1971, 1972, 1973,
1975, 1977.

Scripture quotations identified KJV are from the King
James Version of the Bible.

Library of Congress Cataloging-in-Publication Data
Wilkerson, David R.
  Hungry for more of Jesus : experiencing his presence in
these troubled times / David Wilkerson.
     p.   cm.
  ISBN 0–8007–9200–9 (pbk.) : $9.99
  1. Christian life—1960–   2. Jesus Christ—Person and
offices.   3. Consolation.   I. Title.
BV4501.2.W5199   1992
248.4—dc20   92–186
                                                        CIP

A Chosen Book
Copyright © 1992 by David Wilkerson
Chosen Books are published by Fleming H. Revell
a division of Baker Book House Company
P.O. Box 6287, Grand Rapids, MI 49516-6287

ISBN: 0-8007-9200-9

Sixth printing, June 1993

Printed in the United States of America

To
Scott and Joy Sawyer

Precious lovers of Jesus Christ
Who spent many prayerful hours
Helping edit this book.
They share my hunger for more of Jesus.

CONTENTS

Contents

PREFACE

I have in my library twelve volumes by J. B. Stoney, a devout writer among Plymouth Brethren. Every volume centers on Christ—thousands upon thousands of pages extolling the beauty of our Lord and His ministry as *A Man in Glory*. In devouring these precious books, I find myself continually humbled and challenged by this brother who has written so much on the single subject of the glory of Christ.

In recent years I have been preaching more and more about my blessed Savior and praying much for a greater revelation of His grace and glory. Never in all my years of preaching have I been so hungry for more of Him. The Holy Spirit has not failed to satisfy that growing hunger, and now He has enabled me to share with the Body of Christ a single volume entirely about Jesus.

If you, too, hunger for more of Jesus, you will find some fragments here to feed your soul. I would expect that only those who have been recently awakened by the Holy Spirit to a new hunger and thirst for Christ and His holiness will take the time to read this book. You have to really be *Hungry for More of Jesus* to come to the table and eat. This is not for "fast food" Christians in a hurry—but for those who are learning to wait upon the Lord for manna from heaven.

David Wilkerson

SECTION 1

FEEDING ON CHRIST

1

THE BREAD OF GOD

The Church of Jesus Christ today has been experiencing history's worst spiritual drought. Multitudes of starving sheep are crying out to their shepherds for some life-giving food, something that will sustain them in these troubled times. Yet all too often they are not given even a *scrap* of something spiritual! They leave God's house empty, unsatisfied and weak. And they have grown weary of trudging back to an empty table time after time.

This is not what God intended for His people—and it grieves Him to see it. God has provided bread for the whole world. And the bread He offers is more than mere sustenance; it is food for life in its fullest measure—the "abundant life" Jesus spoke of.

What is this bread of God that we hunger for so desperately? Jesus gave us the answer. He said, "The bread of God is He who comes down from heaven and gives life to the world" (John 6:33). In other words, *Jesus Himself is the answer!* Like the manna sent to sustain life for the children of Israel in the wilderness, Jesus is the Bread of God for us—the gift sent to sustain life for us today and every day.

The Bread of God, when eaten daily, produces a quality of life that Jesus Himself enjoyed. Christ participated in a life that flowed directly from His heavenly Father—a life, He said, that ought also to quicken us: "I live because of the Father, so he who feeds on Me will live because of Me" (John 6:57).

This bread is the very thing that modern Christianity lacks—yet desperately needs. And it is my earnest prayer that this book will help meet the spiritual hunger many are sensing in their lives.

This spiritual famine has continued for years. You see, the further a person strays from Jesus, the Source of all life, the more death seeps into him. In the same way, churches and ministries also die when they lose touch with that life-giving flow. Many of them, in fact, have been slowly decaying for some time. That is why so many disillusioned saints cry out to God, yearning for a church that has some life. It is why most young people refer to their churches as "dead."

The prophet Amos spoke of a day when "fair virgins and strong young men [would] faint from thirst" (Amos 8:13). He cried out,

> "Behold, the days are coming," says the Lord God, "that I will send a famine on the land, not a famine of bread, nor a thirst for water, but of hearing the words of the Lord. They shall wander . . . they shall run to and fro, seeking the word of the Lord, but shall not find it."
>
> Amos 8:11–12

Many Christians are offended when they are told that God sends such a famine of the true Word. And, granted, there is much vigorous preaching and teaching today that is called "revelation." Bibles are more visible than ever. Multitudes flock to hear their favorite preachers and teachers. Some even say this period of Christian history is a day of revival, a glorious time of Gospel light and new truth. Yet if what is being offered to God's people is not the Bread of God from heaven, then it is not true spiritual food. It will not produce life. Instead, it will cause terrible spiritual starvation.

Indeed, starvation abounds right in God's house today. The famine is driving believers from the church to find something that will satisfy their inner needs. Now churches are being overrun with adultery, divorce, "Christian" rock and roll, unbiblical psychology and New Age gospels. Many Christian young people are turning to drugs and sex to try to find fulfillment.

That is because much of what is heard from pulpits today is at best pleasurable pabulum. The sermons are not meaty and not hard to swallow. In fact, they are "fun"! The stories are well-told, the applications easy and practical, and nothing said ever offends anyone. No one has a problem taking along a non-Christian spouse or friend on Sunday because they won't be embarrassed. They won't be confronted about sin. No hot coals from God's altar will burn their consciences, no flaming arrows of conviction from the pulpit will drive them to their knees. No prophetic finger will point straight into their hearts and thunder, "Thou art the man!" And if the hammer does come down against sin, the blow is quickly softened.

It is astonishing but true: The most convenient and conscience-easing place to hide from the flaming eyes of a holy God is inside a dead church. Its preachers serve more as pallbearers than apostles of life. Instead of guiding starving believers to the abundant life Jesus offers, they give soft assurances that try to ease the hunger: "All is well. You have done everything you need to do. Don't bother about feeding on the Bread of God by abiding in prayer, or dusting off your Bibles, or aligning your hearts with His."

Some preachers protest that, far from dead, their churches are full of glorious praise and worship to God. Yet not all exuberant, emotion-stirring churches are necessarily full of life either. Worship from unclean lips is actually an abomination to God. Praise that flows from hearts full of adultery, lust or pride is a stench in God's nostrils. Christian banners held high by sin-stained hands are nothing more than arrogant flauntings of rebellion.

I once heard a minister "prophesy" that a time is coming soon when church meetings will consist of ninety percent praise. Yet if this happens, and even if the praise is heartfelt, that leaves only ten percent for the remainder—which I assume would include the preaching of God's Word. Yet won't we grow spiritually weak if we shout and praise, but do not eat the Bread of God? Does this mean we have reached the place to which the children of Israel came when they complained, "Our appetite is gone. There is nothing . . . except this manna" (Numbers 11:6, NASB)? Could it possibly be that we are bored with sitting at the precious table of the Lord?

We must understand that true praise comes only from thankful hearts—hearts that overflow with the pure life of Jesus Christ!

The apostle John heard a voice crying from the throne room of God, "Give praise to our God, all you His bond-servants, you who fear Him, the small and the great" (Revelation 19:5, NASB). These bondservants were rejoicing and giving glory to God. They had walked as faithful followers who prepared themselves as His Bride (verse 7). And they ate the Bread of God faithfully and reverently because they were in awe of its life-giving power.

How many Christians today fully understand what takes place when we partake of the Bread of God, eating Christ's body and drinking His blood? Christ's pure and all-powerful life-force, when fully infused into the spiritual man or woman, works to expel and destroy all that is of the flesh and the devil. Nothing can drive the cancer of sin from us but this flood of divine life!

The Holy Remnant

The old adage is true: You are what you eat. Jesus said His flesh should be our meat, our staple diet: "Unless you eat the flesh of the Son of Man and drink His blood, you have no life in you" (John 6:53).

The Jews could not comprehend such a thought, and "many of His disciples went back and walked with Him no more" (verse 66). They said, "This is a hard saying; who can understand it?" (verse 60). Even today those who restrict the eating of the Lord's body to the Communion table do not understand what Jesus meant. The reason we observe the Lord's Supper is to remind us that He became our source of life through death. And yet the Communion supper is more than symbolic; the more we come to eat and drink of Christ, the more of His life we will see demonstrated in us. We have an open invitation from heaven to come to His table, to eat and become strong.

I know a number of followers are doing just that! In the midst of a generation of hireling shepherds and pabulum-fed followers, a holy, Levitical priesthood is rising forth in the land today. These are servants and handmaidens who desire to become shepherds after the Lord's heart. And the Spirit has anointed them to lead a separated people who will follow them into the fullness of Christ.

These believers are consumed with love for the Lord, stripped of all pride and worldly ambition, burning with the zeal of holiness. Their numbers are few but growing. They have no food other than Christ, because they know there is no other source of life. They burst with life because they have come diligently and often to the table of the Lord. They love according to the truth, and they are fearless. They denounce sin without apology, tearing down idols and strongholds. And they do all this to bring freedom to their brothers and sisters—to produce in them a hunger for the reality of Christ Jesus and to teach them how to feed on Him.

This holy remnant in the land today worships the Lord in spirit and in truth. They are more enamored of Jesus than of His blessings and gifts. They praise Him with clean hands and pure hearts because the Holy Spirit has taught them that Christ's body will never be offered as food to the unclean. The Holy Spirit will not permit the Bread of God to be brought forth wherever people are holding onto lusts and idols. Yet, tragically, many today still eat at the table of demons, serving their own lustful appetites, and then attempt to come to the Lord's table to feast with the righteous. This leads only to spiritual sickness and death because these deceived ones do not discern the true Bread of God.

These sickly sheep have become so spiritually weak and diseased by sin that they cannot eat strong meat. Instead, they prefer to nibble at the husks of ear-tickling teachings. They gravitate toward lightness and entertainment rather than the genuine Word. Their spiritual appetites have become dull as a result of eating too much junk food.

Take television as just one prime example. Few activities lure Christians as much as this one. Television is a particularly insidious form of idolatry—one that I find myself crying out against more and more as I see our nation's spiritual starvation. What is much of television programming today if not a satanic dinner spread? One network's radio advertisement asked viewers to tune in to a particular TV program "to get a good dose of greed, lust and passion—as you like it." Whatever we Christians might call it, television producers themselves call TV by its true name: a fountain of lust! Yet, even knowing this, literally millions of Christians sit in front of their televisions hour after hour, day after day, taking in a steady diet of garbage that must grieve the heart of God!

Nothing could be clearer to me than God's grief over this—not television itself, but Christians' addiction to it! It is a flaunted outrage against a holy God. The Holy Spirit mourns over the multitudes of spiritually blinded believers who refuse to obey His inner promptings to quit drinking from this filthy cistern. If Jeremiah could witness this sad spectacle—millions of God's people lolling in front of the TV every Sunday, drinking in lust, crime and greed, instead of sitting in God's house to eat His Bread—the prophet would weep and wail. He would cry out from the Lord: "My people have changed their Glory for what does not profit. . . . They have forsaken Me, the fountain of living waters, and hewn themselves cisterns—broken cisterns that can hold no water" (Jeremiah 2:11, 13).

How jealous we must make the Lord! We give our time so generously to eat at the table of His enemies—TV is just one example—but we abandon and ignore His table. Oh, how He would love to have that time to feed us the true Bread of Life! Isn't it past time to overturn the table of the devil in our lives? To enter the prayer closet and feast on the true Bread of God? To rid our lives and homes of everything that stains and pollutes our spiritual minds? We need to ask ourselves honestly: At whose table will we be seated when the Redeemer comes suddenly to Zion?

Bread of Strength

I once spent weeks before the Lord, weeping and crying out to Him for a message of comfort and hope for all the hurting believers who write to our ministry at Times Square Church. And, as we work here in New York City with addicts, alcoholics and the homeless, I have prayed, "Lord, everywhere I look I see pain, sorrow, grief and trouble. What message can I possibly send to those in such dire need? What is Your word to them? Surely You care for these precious people. Surely You long to bring them a word that can set them free."

The Lord has given a word, and it is this: He has provided a way to strengthen every child of His to resist the enemy. This strength comes only from eating the Bread sent down from heaven. And our spiritual health and strength depend on getting this Bread into us.

Listen carefully once more to the words of Jesus: "I live because of the Father, so he who feeds on Me will live because of Me." Jesus was in such close communion with the Father, and was so committed to doing only His will, that the Father's words became His very food and drink each day. Jesus was sustained daily by hearing and seeing what the Father wanted—and this was the result of spending much time alone with Him.

Christ told His disciples, "I have food to eat of which you do not know. . . . My food is to do the will of Him who sent Me, and to finish His work" (John 4:32, 34). He also instructed them, "Do not labor for the food which perishes, but for the food which endures to everlasting life, which the Son of Man will give you" (John 6:27). We dare not miss this secret of strength: Even as Christ lived by the Father, so must we receive our life by feeding on Christ.

A dear 86-year-old man wrote to our ministry, telling how he nurses and cares for his crippled wife. They are too poor to afford a nursing home, and he is worried that he might die, leaving no one to care for her. To this man I say, don't despair! Look up, and drink in Christ's presence. Let the Holy Spirit feed you the manna of heaven. Call on Him—He hears the most feeble cry. And He promises to feed you Himself. He will enter your innermost being with renewed light and life. God said that Jesus is our Bread of Life, from whom we live and receive our sustenance. So trust Him by feeding on Christ—and He will give you strength!

A farmer's wife in Montana wrote that she is angry, perplexed and at the end of her rope because the family farm is about to go bankrupt. Her husband has tried hard but their situation seems dark and hopeless, and no one seems to care. I say to that beloved sister, stay at the Lord's table! Go back to your source of life—the Bread of God!

The writer of Hebrews addressed a people of God who "joyfully accepted the plundering of [their] goods, knowing . . . [they had] a better and an enduring possession . . . in heaven" (Hebrews 10:34). I say along with this writer, "Therefore do not cast away your confidence, which has great reward" (verse 35). Don't leave the table of the Lord and sulk in some dark corner of despair. Wait on Him until you are satisfied—you will find at His table all you need for life and godliness. No one can take that eternal, life-giving Bread away from you. Live by Him! Eat Christ and overcome!

I say to the divorced, the unemployed, the lonely, the parents who grieve over lost children, the sin-bound who want to be free: Have you been looking for help in the wrong places? Do what you know to do: Run back to the Lord's presence and seek Him with all your heart! Go back to eating the right spiritual food, and throw out all the junk. You will find all the power and strength you need as His life comes into you through the Bread of God.

I rejoice with those who have reason to rejoice, and I weep with those who weep. Yet at times I believe I hear the Spirit whispering to me, *Don't grieve with Christians who have forsaken My table. Don't weep over them or let their problems burden you. They do not pray anymore or read My Word, though they waste hours recklessly on themselves. They have forgotten Me day after day. They will go on hurting until they return and eat the Bread that I have provided to heal and strengthen them.*

Our ministry also receives letters from Christians who have endured great affliction but who eat God's Bread daily. Many of these believers have only grown stronger, with an increasing sense of

God's presence in their lives. In the midst of their testing they have turned to the Lord with all their hearts. They have sought Him in their troubles—and He has heard their cry and satisfied their hungry souls, giving them what they need to endure the hard times. God has raised them above their problems—until knowing Christ has become more important to them than finding relief. They live on Christ literally, because they have discovered Him to be their mighty source of strength. And one day they will come forth as pure gold, having been tried by fire. They will be totally purified of self and pride. Like Christ, their only desire will be to do the will of the Father and to finish His work.

The Bread of God is dispensed daily, just as manna was to the Israelites. The Bible says God gave His people manna to humble them (Deuteronomy 8:16). They were not humbled because it was poor man's food, for it was in fact "angels' food" (see Psalm 78:25). No, they were humbled because they had to seek this food on a daily basis. It reminded them that God held the key to the cupboard. They were forced to wait upon Him and acknowledge continually that He alone was their source.

Christians today are humbled in the same fashion. God is telling us that what we ate of Christ yesterday will not supply our need for today. We must admit we will starve spiritually and become weak and helpless without a fresh, daily supply of heavenly Bread. We must come to the Lord's table often. We must be diligent to keep the feast. We must make up our minds that the time will never come in our lives when we will have more than one day's supply of strength.

For those of us who love Jesus and desire to count ourselves as part of that faithful remnant, I can promise one thing: Famines do not last forever. God will again visit His people. As we will see in the next chapter, He wants to satisfy us completely. He wants to give us the abundant life we long for. He longs to meet every sincere heart that is *hungry for more of Jesus.*

∼ 2 ∼
WINNING CHRIST

Do you know if you have won your Lord's heart? Do you know that if you hunger after Him you will have a desire to win His heart? The apostle Paul stated that this was his purpose in renouncing his past life:

> I count all things but loss for the excellency of the knowledge of Christ Jesus my Lord: for whom I have suffered the loss of all things, and do count them but dung, *that I may win Christ.*
>
> Philippians 3:8, KJV

Paul was completely captivated by his Lord. Why would he feel the need to "win" Christ? Christ already had revealed Himself clearly, and not just *to* the apostle but *in* his life. Yet, even so, Paul felt compelled to win Christ's heart and affection.

Paul's entire being—his ministry, life and very purpose for living—was focused only on pleasing his Master and Lord. All else was rubbish to him, even "good" things. I believe one of the reasons Paul never married was to give himself more time to care for the things of the Lord (see 1 Corinthians 7:32). And he urged others in the same direction, "that you may walk worthy of the Lord, fully pleasing Him" (Colossians 1:10).

Is this scriptural, you may ask, this idea of winning the heart of Jesus? Aren't we already the objects of God's love? Indeed, His benevolent love extends to all mankind. But there is another kind of love that few Christians ever experience. It is an affectionate love with Christ such as occurs between a husband and wife.

This love is expressed in the Song of Solomon. In that book, Solomon is portrayed as a type of Christ and in one passage, the Lord speaks of His bride this way:

> You have ravished my heart . . . my spouse; you have ravished my heart with one look of your eyes, with one link of your necklace. How fair is your love . . . my spouse! How much better than wine is your love . . . !
>
> Song of Solomon 4:9–10

Later He says, "Turn your eyes away from me, for they have overcome me" (6:5). His bride responds, "I am my beloved's, and his desire is toward me" (7:10).

The bride of Christ will consist of a holy people who long to be so pleasing to their Lord, and who live so obediently and so separated from all other things, that Christ's heart will be ravished. The word *ravish* in this passage means to "unheart" or to "steal my heart." The King James Version of the above passage says that Christ's heart is ravished with just "one eye." I believe that "one eye" is the singleness of a mind focused on Christ alone. This singleminded devotion to Christ—and also the symbolic love between husband and wife—is expressed in another book of the Bible: Ruth. It is the story of a converted maiden who won the heart of her earthly lord. I see it as a prophetic story, a message that speaks powerfully to us today, for we win Christ in the same way that Ruth won her master, Boaz.

Yet as I researched this idea, poring through all my commentaries, I could not find a single writer who saw this spiritual and prophetic meaning in the book of Ruth. Only one writer even suggested that, since Ruth was a Moabite, God may be telling us something about the Gentiles being "grafted into the vine." But there is much more to this story than just historic significance. I believe we need to look at this beautiful story more closely because it teaches us a great deal about how we are fed by seeking to win His heart.

The story of Ruth begins with these words: "There was a famine in the land" (Ruth 1:1). This famine represents the same famine that the Church has been experiencing today: the absence of God's presence, a hungering for the true Bread of God. Because of the famine, the Israelite Elimelech took his wife, Naomi, and their two sons and fled the land of Judah for Moab. Elimelech later died there and Naomi's two sons married heathen wives, Orpah and Ruth. They all remained in Moab for another ten years.

But Moab was a place of idolatry. It represented the congregation of the wicked, the seat of the scornful. In fact, the name *Moab* means fornication. Moab himself, after whom the region was named, was born of an incestuous relationship between Lot and one of his daughters. It was he who seduced Israel at Shittim in the wilderness, and afterward 24,000 died from a plague.

God forbade the Israelites to marry Moabite women, for "surely they will turn away your hearts after their gods" (1 Kings 11:2). As I pointed out in the last chapter, the same thing happens in the spiritual realm today when a famine of God's Word occurs: God's people turn toward the world, yielding to the seduction of idolatry and mixing with the ungodly. The famine in the Church has driven believers to Moab, the place of idolatry. And, as Naomi learned when she lost her sons there, *Moab is a place where young men die!*

Back in Judah, however, the famine was finally over. Word came to Naomi that God was once again visiting His people with plenty of bread. Suddenly memories of past blessings flooded Naomi's soul and she began to yearn for the holy place where she once dwelled. She was sick of Moab and its idolatry and death. So "she arose with her daughters-in-law that she might return" (Ruth 1:6).

Ruth and Orpah said good-bye to parents, friends and family.

They told their lifelong loved ones that they would be gone for good: They were going with Naomi to Judah, a place where God was visiting His people!

We can see the parallel in our world today: Some believers have resided in a contemporary Moab—lethargy, coldness, worldly pleasure and success. Yet in the midst of these, a holy remnant has persevered. They have endured the self-exaltation of TV evangelists, the sordid sensuality in God's house, the foolishness in the pulpit and mockery by backslidden Christians. These hungry ones have prayed, fasted and interceded, and now the Lord has heard their cry.

Why is Times Square Church, and others like it, packed with hungry seekers? Because word has gotten out that God is visiting His people in these places! People have heard that a word from God is coming forth. *Yes, the famine is over.* God has sent bread from heaven. And if you have not yet tasted the heavenly manna, then get out of Moab and go back to where God is visiting His people!

This is exactly what Naomi's two daughters-in-law planned to do. You see, Naomi's name means "grace." And following their mother-in-law was a way of following God's grace. It represented a move away from living for the world and a move toward living by the grace of the Lord. They were being drawn by the Spirit of God, attracted by the news of His visitation. And today in the same way thousands are heading home, back to the fullness of Christ— away from the hype, compromise, halfheartedness and emptiness of a gospel of ease and prosperity.

The sad thing is that many who plan to return to God stop at the border. They don't break loose totally, they don't pay the price. I have seen this happen to hundreds of people in our church: They start out with great fervor, claiming to be hungry. But then they get hung up on the border between Moab and Judah and turn back to their old ways. Likewise, in Scripture, when Orpah and Ruth reached the border they faced a decision: Would they follow Naomi—that is, God's grace—into the fullness of the Lord? Their names offer a clue to the answer: *Orpah* means "stiff-neckedness." *Ruth* means "friend, companion."

Going Back and Going On

A confrontation took place at the border. Naomi decided to test the two younger women's commitment. For Orpah and Ruth, the decision to go on would require more than emotions and mere words. Naomi could guarantee them no rewards for following, no prosperity, ease or success; she could offer only a clear vision of the high cost ahead. She described her homeland as a place of suffering and poverty, a land that offered nothing of earthly goods; they would have to exist only on a walk of faith. The picture was so bleak that Naomi encouraged them both to return to their own mothers' houses "that you may find rest" (Ruth 1:9).

The picture Naomi presented is indeed the gospel of God's grace: suffering, self-denial, the cross. And Orpah and Ruth both remained steadfast—at least on the surface: "They lifted up their voices and wept. And they said to her, 'Surely we will return with you to your people' " (Ruth 1:9–10).

You have probably guessed from Orpah's name that, in spite of her river of tears and her strong words about pressing on, she would drop out and return to her idolatry. Outwardly she was broken and tender, and she seemed to want to be part of the move back to God. But her heart was gripped powerfully by her love for her old circle of friends and family; she didn't know this idol remained in her soul. Orpah wept at the border because she was torn between two loves. She sincerely wanted to go on, and she loved the precious fellowship of the other two women—but she had not cut the ties to Moab.

Tears are never enough. Naomi knew this and put the two younger women to a final test. Naomi said, "Turn back, my daughters; why will you go with me? Are there still sons in my womb, that they may be your husbands? Turn back, my daughters, go" (Ruth 1:11–12). I believe Naomi saw into Orpah's heart, into her inner struggle.

Naomi probably thought to herself, *The poor child! She thinks she wants the Lord's fullness, but she is still charmed by this world. She would be miserable if she went on, because she would always be looking back.* So Naomi told Orpah, "Go your way!"

Orpah then must have reached a decision in her heart. She had probably asked herself, *Is this the only option? Rejection, poverty and separation from all I've ever known? No! I'll go back to Moab and serve God my way. I'll still love these saints, but I've got to get on with my life.* The Bible says, "They lifted up their voices and wept again; and Orpah kissed her mother-in-law" (Ruth 1:14). An original manuscript adds to the sentence, "and went back."

Perhaps as some of you read this right now, you may be thinking of kissing your brothers and sisters in Christ good-bye. Something in your heart could be pulling you away, perhaps a circle of old friends or the lure of old habits. Orpah went "back to her people and to her gods" (Ruth 1:15). Your heart, too, can be gripped by an idol from your past, something you can't let go of.

Yet there is no middle ground for the Christian! The line has been drawn and we can move in only one of two directions: either forward toward Judah, or backward toward Moab. Orpah turned back and from this point on in Scripture, she is never heard from again. She faded away into the shadows of idolatry, having nothing more to do with God's work or eternal Kingdom. Now God's great concern was with Ruth.

Naomi tried one last time to discourage Ruth, saying in verse 15, "Return after your sister-in-law." In other words: "Quick, Ruth! If you hurry you can catch up with Orpah. Why don't you go and follow after your own desires?" But Ruth wouldn't let go: She "clung" to Naomi (Ruth 1:14). This suggests a picture of a maiden on her knees with her arms around her master's waist, as if she will never let go.

Ruth wanted God! She wanted to take part in the great visitation of the Lord, and only death could stop her now.

Ruth said: "Entreat me not to leave you, or to turn back from following after you; for wherever you go, I will go; and wherever you lodge, I will lodge; your people shall be my people, and your God, my God. Where you die, I will die, and there will I be buried. The Lord do so to me, and more also, if anything but death parts you and me." When she saw that she was determined to go with her, she stopped speaking to her.

Ruth 1:16–18

Little did Ruth know that by making the choice to go on, she placed herself under the sheltering wings of Jehovah. And, more importantly, as soon as she crossed over the border with Naomi, she was on the road to winning Christ. There was no signpost to tell her, but we know where the road led—straight to the heart of Jesus.

Soon, Ruth and Naomi came to the place of blessing, arriving during the beginning of the harvest season. They were poor and almost stripped bare, not knowing where their next meal would come from. Then young Ruth said, "Let me go to the field and glean."

In those days, only the very poor did such work. The Law commanded field owners not to harvest the four corners of their fields or to glean the rest—that is, gather up the grain missed by the reapers—but to leave that excess available for the poor (see Leviticus 19:9–10).

At this point, it looked as though Ruth had made a poor bargain. Her devotion had led her all the way to the place of God's visitation, yet now she had to sweat over a minimum-wage job. She was below the poverty line, with no future in sight.

I urge you to take a good look at Ruth, because this is how you may end up if you break loose from the world and go all the way with God. This was the cross of the apostle Paul until he died:

We have been made a spectacle to the world, both to angels and to men. We are fools for Christ's sake. . . . [We] both hunger and thirst, and we are poorly clothed . . . and homeless. And we labor, working with our own hands. Being reviled . . . persecuted . . . defamed. . . [we] have been made as the filth of the world.

1 Corinthians 4:9–13

Yet Paul had the audacity to say, "Therefore I urge you, imitate me" (1 Corinthians 4:16)! He said this with good reason, and it is the reason we can't feel sorry for someone like Ruth: because she was just about to win Christ!

"She . . . went and gleaned in the field after the reapers. And she happened to come to the part of the field belonging to Boaz, who was of the family of Elimelech" (Ruth 2:3).

The writer of this story must have chuckled when he wrote that Ruth "happened" to end up in the field of Boaz, her kinsman-redeemer. This was far from accidental. It was, rather, the clear leading of the Holy Spirit, because from the moment Ruth crossed the border and trusted her entire life to God's call, she was led supernaturally by Him.

The scenario must have looked something like this: Ruth, with a song in her heart, passed by many fields. Then a sudden urge within compelled her to turn right and start gleaning on the north end of a particular field. A few hours later, Boaz got inspired to check on the harvesting. He looked over the fields and saw numerous young men cutting sheaves and poor maidens gleaning behind them. But then he stopped, because his gaze was held by Ruth. "Whose young woman is this?" he asked. He was smitten on the spot. She gleaned for only half a day before she caught the eye of her master! That great man walked over to her and said, "Do not go to glean in another field . . . but stay close [in the company of] my young women" (Ruth 2:8). He promised that no one would bother her, and said that when she was thirsty she should go and drink from what the harvesters had drawn. Later he told his harvesters to drop handfuls of grain on purpose for her to find.

Why did Boaz say this to Ruth? *Because he was ravished by her.* She had stolen his heart and he had to have her near him. And what attracted Boaz to Ruth in the first place? Ruth asked that question of him herself: "Why should you take notice of me since I am a stranger?"

Boaz answered that he had heard of all she had done for her mother-in-law, and how she left her own land to join a new people.

"[May] a full reward be given you by the Lord God of Israel, under whose wings you have come for refuge" (Ruth 2:12). Boaz was drawn to her because she had come to trust the covering wings of God.

We Become the Apple of Christ's Eye

Do you see the parallel? Boaz represents Christ, our Kinsman-Redeemer. The moment we walk away from all other loves, the moment we let go of all former idols, old friends and old ways, Christ's eyes fall upon us. That is when we win Christ. We lose the world and its fleeting glory and passing pleasures, but we win His eternal love.

And when we win His heart, we also win His favor. Never again will we suffer hunger or thirst in our inner man. He will lead us and provide for us in miraculous ways. Like Ruth, who ran home to tell Naomi all the exciting things that happened to her, we will run to the family of God and share miracle after miracle of how the Lord is supplying all our needs. Each of us will end up saying, "Who am I to be so blessed?"

This was only the beginning of Ruth's blessings. At the end of the harvest Naomi directed Ruth to take part in a custom of the times. In that day servants would sleep at their masters' feet in perpendicular fashion, fully clothed, in order to warm them. If the master was a near relative, it was his duty to redeem, or purchase, this servant's inheritance so that it would not be lost. The kinsman signified that he would do this by taking a cloth or covering and putting it over the servant's shoulders, saying, in effect, "I will be your covering."

Naomi told Ruth to go to the threshing floor that night where Boaz would be winnowing barley; and, after he had lain down, she was to uncover his feet, lie down there and do whatever Boaz told her. So that night, Ruth did as Naomi had directed. And when Boaz awoke to find her there, he was eminently pleased:

> "Blessed are you of the Lord, my daughter! For you have shown more kindness at the end than at the beginning, in that you did not go after young men, whether poor or rich. And now, my daughter,

do not fear. I will do for you all that you request, for all the people of my town know that you are a virtuous woman."

Ruth 3:10–11

Think of what Boaz was saying: "I will do for you all that you have desired." Every desire of Ruth's heart would be granted, because she had been faithful. She had not turned her eyes to wealth, success or glamour—she had wanted only him. And in turn, her redeemer-kinsman said to her, "I can trust you; your love is true. You won't leave me for others, no matter how attractive they are. You will be mine only and I will be yours only."

So at the gate of Bethlehem, before ten witnesses, Boaz redeemed Ruth's inheritance. He satisfied all claims to her and her possessions and acquired her as his wife. The mighty man of wealth married the lowly servant.

This is indeed the work of the cross: Jesus has cleared all claims that the devil has on us or our inheritances. We are completely free to be espoused to Christ!

After their marriage Ruth gave birth to a son. His name was Obed, and he became the great-grandfather of David, the seed of Christ. This servant, Ruth, has a place in the very lineage of our Messiah.

Did Ruth win Christ? Why, Christ became her very life! In the same way today, we win Christ by the choices we make that are pleasing to Him, decisions that prove our faithfulness to feed only on Him. If we love Him unreservedly, hungering for Him continuously, we will remember Him in every choice. We will ask ourselves, "Will this please Him? Will it make Him say to the angels, 'See, My love has left all else for Me'?"

If we truly hunger for Jesus, we will desire to win His heart—and then to *know* His heart. We will abandon ourselves completely to Him and rest peacefully under His almighty care.

~ 3 ~
ANSWERING THE CALL TO GRIEF

Just as Ruth teaches us about sharing the Lord's joy, the prophet Samuel teaches us about sharing His grief.

What does grief in our hearts have to do with hungering for Jesus? If we are truly going to hunger for Him, we will have to know His heart and come out against the sins that break it. This is not always easy, but I am convinced that the only way to experience the fullness of joy in Christ is to share in His grief as well. Scripture says that in the days of Noah,

> The Lord saw that the wickedness of man was great in the earth, and that every intent of the thoughts of his heart was only evil continually. And the Lord was sorry that He had made man on the earth, and He was grieved in His heart.
>
> Genesis 6:5–6

God indeed grieves over sin, and those who walk truly with Him will also enter into that grief.

The Hebrew word for *grief* here means "cut to the heart." It signifies hurt or pain. The wickedness of mankind hurt God deeply and caused great pain to His heart. Isaiah said of Christ, "He is . . . a Man of sorrows and acquainted with grief. . . . Surely He has borne our griefs and carried our sorrows" (Isaiah 53:3–4). Christ Himself entered into the very hurt and pain of the heavenly Father—that is, the grief caused by the sin of mankind.

This grief is present in the lives of men throughout the Bible. King David discovered the glory of joy in Jehovah God. But David's joy was born out of great grief over the transgressions among the Lord's people. He said, "I beheld the transgressors, and was grieved; because they kept not thy word" (Psalm 119:158, KJV). "Do not I hate them, O Lord, that hate thee? and am not I grieved with those that rise up against thee?" (Psalm 139:21, KJV). David hated what God hated, and he grieved over the things that grieved God.

The prophet Amos shared God's grief over a backslidden people who lounged in ease, ignoring the impending hour of judgment. He cried out against those "who are at ease in Zion . . . [who] are not grieved for the affliction of Joseph" (Amos 6:1, 6). These people played the music of their pleasure and drank the wine of selfishness, but they had no grief over the ruin all around them (see Amos 6:1–6). The word Amos used to describe their lack of grief is *sickened.* He was actually saying to them, "The sin and ruin among God's people does not sicken or disgust you, because you have become blinded by sin and the good life you now enjoy."

Nehemiah was grieved because he saw the evil that had infiltrated the house of God. A backslidden priesthood had brought terrible compromise into the Lord's house, and only Nehemiah understood the depth of the iniquity and the awful consequences it would bring upon the people (see Nehemiah 13:1–9).

During this time the high priest Eliashib, whose name in Hebrew suggests "unity through compromise," had set up residence in the Temple for Tobiah, an Ammonite prince. By law, no Ammonite was permitted to set foot in the Temple. But Eliashib allowed Tobiah (whose name means "prosperity, pleasure, good life") to live there. The high priest made God's house a dwelling place for a heathen! Thus, a corrupt ministry was now in league with paganism. "Eliashib the priest, having authority over the storerooms of the house of our God, was allied with Tobiah" (Nehemiah 13:4). The people of God yearned for prosperity and the good life, and Tobiah was only too willing to teach them the materialistic path of idolatry.

Nehemiah saw the evil that was being sponsored by a soft-on-sin priesthood:

> And I came to Jerusalem and discovered the evil that Eliashib had done for Tobiah, in preparing a room for him in the courts of the house of God. And it grieved me bitterly; therefore I threw all the household goods of Tobiah out of the room. Then I commanded them to cleanse the rooms; and I brought back into them the articles of the house of God.
>
> Nehemiah 13:7–9

Nehemiah was not acting on impulse or legalistic tradition. Rather, he was seeing through God's eyes, feeling as God felt, discerning the evil of the cancerous growth of compromise in God's house. If more ministers today understood the dangers of fleshly entertainment and the lust for materialism, they would grieve over them as Nehemiah did and cast them out of their churches. O Lord, give us a body of preachers and parishioners who are sick of sin and who will take a stand against it! Give us people with enough discernment to see the depth and horror of the compromise that has crept into God's house!

In the New Testament, Paul also grieved over the backsliding of God's people. He warned,

> Many walk, of whom I have told you often, and now tell you even weeping, that they are the enemies of the cross of Christ: whose end is destruction, whose God is their belly, and whose glory is in their shame—who set their mind on earthly things.
>
> Philippians 3:18–19

The Greek meaning for Paul's *weeping* here is loud or piercing sobbing from a broken heart. As Paul saw those Christians turn aside to embrace earthly things and reject the reproach of the cross, his heart broke to the point that he literally shook with God's grief. This was not silent despair or a resigned sigh; it was the loud, piercing, heartbroken cry of a man entering into God's own grief for His wayward children.

But as I mentioned earlier, the one man—with the exception of Christ—who was called more than any other to express God's grief was Samuel. He was actually called to the ministry of grief. The grief he bore was not his own or that of humanity; rather, it was the deep and unfathomable grief of God.

The Ministry of Grief

In the years before Samuel was born, God's people had fallen away from Him into idolatry and internal decay. God was profoundly grieved over their backslidden condition, and He had no one who could express it to the people. The Lord was about to remove His glory from His house at Shiloh, and the ministers who stood before His altar at that time did not even know it. How sad to be so deaf, dumb and blind right at the hour of judgment! Israel was corrupt, the priesthood was adulterous and the established, organized ministry was totally blind.

Eli, who was the priest of the Temple at the time, represents the decaying religious systems with all their self-interest and only token disdain for sin. Just as the people had grown soft by easy living, Eli himself had become fat and lazy about the things of God. He was simply going through the motions, not only of his priesthood but of his fatherhood as well.

His sons Hophni and Phinehas represent the ongoing ministry of tradition. These two young priests never did have an encounter with God. They knew nothing of hungering for God, of hearing from heaven, of burning passionately to experience the glory and presence of the Lord. They were consumed with lust and hardened by sin.

We do not have to look so far back to see the kind of religious system that guards and even encourages self-serving ministers. We can just look around us today and see shepherds who do not fast or pray, who look for the best ministerial positions with the highest benefits and the best chance for promotion. Their hearts have never been broken over lost humanity. They know little of suffering. They are the products of cold, dead ritualism; they are not fresh from time spent with God. They say the right things—novel things—and they sound and act professional. But they have no anointing, no holy unction. They do not know the fear and dread of a holy God. And, like Eli's sons, they become sensual, worldly and self-serving. They make themselves "fat with the best of all the offerings of Israel" (1 Samuel 2:29). Hophni and Phinehas became so corrupt that God called them "the sons of Belial," or "sons of Satan." Scripture says of them, "They did not know the Lord" (verse 12).

This is yet another reason why multitudes of evangelical youth today are growing cold and sensual, leading a bored and restless existence: Too many pastors have catered to the sensual desires of these young people. We now face the tragedy of an entire generation's going astray because so few shepherds can show them how to escape the satanic snares of this age.

As may happen with these wayward shepherds, Eli lost all of his spiritual discernment. This is clear through the presence of Hannah, a godly woman who wept bitterly in the house of God at Shiloh. She remained in deep intercession, beseeching the Lord to give her a son. Hannah serves as a type of the interceding holy remnant today who yearn and cry out to God for a fresh word from Him.

"Now Hannah spoke in her heart; only her lips moved, but her voice was not heard. Therefore Eli thought she was drunk" (1 Samuel 1:13). Hannah was in the Spirit, conversing with God, under divine unction and soon to become a channel of renewal in Israel. Yet Eli, the man of God, could not discern this! He totally missed the significance of what was happening at the altar. You have to wonder what had happened to this priest of the Most High. How could he stand at the threshold of a profound new move of

God and yet be so out of touch with the Lord that he mistook the Spirit for the flesh?

The Lord was grieved; He wanted to shake things. He was about to move swiftly. How could He get His message through to this backslidden, corrupt people of Israel? The priest had become so indulgent, comfortable and steeped in tradition that he had not the slightest hint of what God was about to do. The message to us in this passage is clear: God had to go outside the established religious structure to find someone open enough to Him to share His grief.

The Prophecy

As we know from this familiar story, Hannah did conceive and bear a son, Samuel, and she dedicated him to the service of the Lord. Some time after the child went to live with Eli in the Temple, God sent an unnamed prophet to the priest with a message. The word he brought was like an arrow shot directly into the heart of a religious system that had thought itself well-protected. God said to Eli, "You . . . honor your sons more than Me. . . . I will cut off your arm and the arm of your father's house. . . . And all the descendants of your house shall die in the flower of their age" (1 Samuel 2:29, 31, 33).

How had Eli honored his sons more than he had honored his God? By knowing of his sons' wicked behavior and doing nothing about it. When Eli heard, for instance, how his sons flaunted their fornication at the very door of the tabernacle, all he said to them was, "No, my sons! For it is not a good report that I hear. You make the Lord's people transgress" (1 Samuel 2:24). And when they took the meat that was intended for the Lord's offering, he looked the other way. God later confirmed with the young Samuel that this was why He would judge Eli's house: "I have told him that I will judge his house forever for the iniquity which he knows, because his sons made themselves vile, and he did not restrain them" (1 Samuel 3:13).

I believe that a day of judgment is appointed here on earth

anytime ministers of the Gospel know about the sin in their congregations or their families yet refuse to deal with it. They may slap the wrists of the adulterers, the fornicators, the gossips, the self-centered—but they offer no penetrating message of reproof. They are afraid to discipline their spiritual children. But on Judgment Day our Lord will ask, "Why did you not show the people the difference between the holy and the profane?"

Why was Eli so soft on the sins of his boys? Because when they stole the filet mignon before it went into the seething pot, they brought the fresh, red meat to Eli for roasting—and he had grown accustomed to it! If he came down too hard on them, he would have to go back to eating the sodden, boiled meat from the offering that was the priest's portion. He had learned to shut his eyes to all the evil around him in God's house and in his own family.

This is why some preachers are soft on sin: Their appetites have become whetted by the good life. They enjoy the comfort and prestige of large numbers and big buildings. Oh, how subtle compromise is! When something must be addressed, the minister simply utters a limp, "You shouldn't do these evil things." He has no holy thunder, no grief over sin and compromise, no vision like Paul's of the exceeding idolatry of sin, no warnings of divine retribution and judgment. "After all," he says, "people might get offended, stop coming and stop paying the bills. The growth of the church might be hindered."

I have preached in some of these churches and it is a heartbreaking experience. Like Eli, the pastor usually loves God. He is not an evil man, but he *is* a fearful man. He is afraid of the moving of the Holy Spirit, afraid of offending people. He pays lip service to holiness, but he fears dealing too harshly with sin. Divorce is rampant in his church; some people have secret affairs; young people are bound by evil habits.

I have stood in some of these brothers' pulpits calling for repentance, making known the Lord's demand for holiness and warning of His judgment upon sin. Those who have been living in compromise rush forward, weeping, confessing, seeking to be made clean. But when I look at the pastor, I see that he is worried that the service might get out of control. He is afraid people might weep uncontrollably or fall to the floor from conviction as they grieve over their sins. He fears his "new people" won't understand—so he cannot wait to take over the meeting and quiet things down. He comes to the pulpit and whispers sweet reassurances that God loves them all, then reminds everyone of the lateness of the hour and quickly dismisses the gathering. He puts a wet blanket on the Holy Spirit's conviction—and the sin-burdened members go home troubled by what appears to be their pastor's lack of concern.

I leave these kinds of meetings brokenhearted. I ask myself, *Where is the grief over sin? Can't leaders see that these weeping sheep want to allow the conviction of the Holy Ghost to do His cleansing work in them?*

The Samuel Company

Where are the Samuels who have heard the voice of God, who have been awakened by the Holy Spirit and have received a revelation of soon-coming judgments upon a backslidden Church? Why aren't all preachers of the Gospel grieving over the sinful condition of God's house? Why aren't all pastors and evangelists crying out as watchmen on the wall? Scripture says that Samuel was given a vision in which God pronounced the end of a backslidden religious structure, and "Samuel told [Eli] everything, and hid nothing from him" (1 Samuel 3:18). I ask you, pastor: Are you telling it all? Are you holding back, hiding the truth, afraid of offending your people?

Yet in spite of those who are afraid to come forth with the full message for the Church, I believe that the Lord always brings in a "Samuel company" who *will* hear His voice in a time of spiritual decline. This company is made up of men and women who care nothing for tradition, promotion or denominational boundaries. They represent pastors and laypeople who have an ear to hear God's voice and know what grieves Him.

Without question the message of the Samuel company is not a pleasant one. "Samuel was afraid to tell Eli the vision" (verse 15). This vision was overwhelming; but Samuel could not help but share it with the one on whom judgment would fall. God would no longer put up with a form of godliness that did not have the power of holiness.

Yes, God was about to remove His presence from Shiloh, but He would do a glorious new thing in Israel. He said, "I will raise up for Myself a faithful priest who shall do according to what is in My heart and in My mind. I will build him a sure house, and he shall walk before My anointed forever" (1 Samuel 2:35). This verse describes the Samuel company of believers and ministers who share the very heart of God. They know the Lord's mind and His will, and they walk in fear and holiness before Him. The Samuel company is a praying people; it was while Samuel was in prayer that God revealed to him the fearful things to come. And because they are in touch with God they know and share His grief.

God is speaking in these last days to those who are shut in with Him. He reveals His heart to those who hunger and thirst for more of Him—who pant after Him as the deer pants after the water, who have died to every selfish ambition and who have no goal in life but to bring pleasure, glory and joy to His heart. I say this unflinchingly: God will not choose a denomination to deliver His Word to this last generation. He will not call on a committee to hear His voice and ignite the last-day gathering of the remnant. Instead, when the angels of the apocalypse go forth to smite the earth, denominations and religious leaders will be found hard at work protecting their interests and strengthening their authority, drawing up by-laws and making resolutions. But the Samuel company will be found in the secret closet of prayer, seeking their Master's will and sharing His grief over sin.

Samuel, the man God raised up to serve as judge and prophet for the Israelites, bore God's grief over His people to the very end of his ministry. The Bible says Israel eventually lusted after a king so they could be "judge[d] . . . like all the nations" (1 Samuel 8:5). At this Samuel fell on his knees, greatly displeased. God spoke these sad words to him: "Heed the voice of the people in all that they say to you; for they have not rejected you, but they have rejected Me, that I should not reign over them" (1 Samuel 8:7).

Samuel went to the people and warned them of the hardships they would have under a king, how he would conscript their children and take their lands and produce, but the people insisted it was what they wanted. "Make them a king," the Lord said, and their history changed again even as they broke God's heart.

Everywhere you turn now a growing number of God's people are rejecting the Lordship of Christ. They are clamoring to be "like the nations." That is the essence of compromise or mixture: to be just like the world. They are saying, "We want God and the world, too!" They want the world's recognition and prestige, the world's pleasures and the "good life" of luxury. But thank God for the protesting Samuel company! They have heard from God, and they know where all this compromise is going to end. They see the frightful results of apostasy ahead, and like Samuel they sob a piercing, heartrending cry of grief.

With the Grief Comes Joy

Those who weep over sin in the Church and discern her errors are called doomsayers. Many who know them say, "I don't like to be around them. They sound negative and morose and they look so sad." But such onlookers simply do not know these weeping people. They do not understand that those who truly grieve with God are given a leaping heart of joy in Jehovah.

> Although the fig tree shall not bear fruit; neither should there be any provision on the vines; the produce of the olive should fail, and the fields not yield subsistence; the flocks should be cut off from the fold, neither should there be any herd in the stalls. Yet will I leap for joy in Jehovah. I will exult in the God of my salvation. Jehovah my Lord is my strength.
>
> Habakkuk 3:17–19, Spurrell Original Hebrew

Such joy comes from knowing that God will always have a pure ministry through a holy and separated people, even in the most evil of days. These people know that God will honor them with His constant presence. They draw strength from believing in the majesty and power of God, whose judgments are always righteous. With Habakkuk they can say, "Though all else fails, my heart will rejoice in God alone." Even when failure seems to surround them and they see little evidence of fruit, their grief gives way to ecstatic joy because they are near to the heart of the Lord. And, like Paul, this grieving remnant can say, "As sorrowful, yet always rejoicing; as poor, yet making many rich; as having nothing, and yet possessing all things" (2 Corinthians 6:10).

It seems that Samuel had little joy during the disastrous reign of Saul, the chosen king, for he continued to mourn for him (1 Samuel 15:35). Finally the Lord said, "How long will you mourn for Saul, seeing I have rejected him from reigning over Israel? Fill your horn with oil, and go; I am sending you to Jesse the Bethlehemite. For I have provided Myself a king among his sons" (1 Samuel 16:1). This was, of course, the young David, a man who shepherded Israel "according to the integrity of his heart" (Psalm 78:72) and who prefigured the Messiah.

It is, in fact, David's words that encourage us to believe that sharing God's grief will result in rejoicing. Speaking from his own wealth of experiences as one who hungered after the Lord, David said, "Weeping may endure for a night, but joy comes in the morning" (Psalm 30:5).

So may it be for the hungering people today! May we find that our hunger leads to the prayer closet to share His grief, and to the Body of Christ to share His joy.

4

HAVING A PERFECT HEART

Do you know it is possible to walk before the Lord with a perfect heart? If you are hungering for Jesus, you may already be trying— desiring earnestly to obey this command of the Lord.

I want to encourage you: it is possible or God would not have given us such a call. Having a perfect heart has been part of covenant faith from the time God first spoke to Abraham: "I am the Almighty God; walk before me, and be thou perfect" (Genesis 17:1, KJV). Later God reminded the children of Israel, "Thou shalt be perfect with the Lord thy God" (Deuteronomy 18:13, KJV).

In the Old Testament we see that some succeeded. David, for instance, determined in his heart to obey God's command to be perfect. He said, "I will behave wisely in a perfect way. . . . I will walk within my house with a perfect heart" (Psalm 101:2). His son Solomon, however, was one of many to fall short: "His heart was not perfect with the Lord his God, as was the heart of David his father. . . . [He] went not fully after the Lord, as did David his father" (1 Kings 11:4–6, KJV).

In the New Testament we see that God's command for His

people to be perfect is renewed in His Son. Jesus said, "You shall be perfect, just as your Father in heaven is perfect" (Matthew 5:48). Paul said he labored, preaching and teaching, "that we may present every man perfect in Christ Jesus" (Colossians 1:28) and "that you may stand perfect and complete in all the will of God" (4:12). Peter wrote, "The God of all grace, who called us to His eternal glory by Christ Jesus, after you have suffered a while, perfect, establish, strengthen, and settle you" (1 Peter 5:10).

To come to grips with the idea of perfection, we first must understand that perfection does not mean a sinless, flawless existence. People judge by outward appearances, by what they see. But God judges the heart, the unseen motives (1 Samuel 16:7). David had a perfect heart toward God "all the days of his life"—yet David failed the Lord often. In fact, his life was marked forever by adultery and a notorious murder.

No, perfection in the Lord's eyes means something entirely different. It means completeness, maturity. The Hebrew and Greek meanings of *perfection* include "uprightness, having neither spot nor blemish, being totally obedient." It means to finish what has been started, to make a complete performance. John Wesley called this concept of perfection "constant obedience"; that is, a perfect heart is a responsive heart, one that answers quickly and totally all the Lord's wooings, whisperings and warnings. Such a heart says at all times, "Speak, Lord, for Your servant is listening. Show me the path, and I will walk in it."

Some time ago, during the long drive from the Teen Challenge farm in Pennsylvania to New York City, the Lord spoke to my inner man. He said, *There is such a thing as a perfect heart and I want to show you what it is so you can seek after it.* He then showed me three things that distinguish such a heart.

1. A perfect heart is searchable.

The perfect heart cries out with David, "Search me, O God, and know my heart; try me, and know my anxieties; and see if there is any wicked way in me" (Psalm 139:23–24).

God does indeed search our hearts; He said as much to Jeremiah:

"I, the Lord, search the heart" (Jeremiah 17:10). This is also stated in 1 Chronicles 28:9: "The Lord searches all hearts." The Hebrew meaning for this phrase is, "I penetrate, I examine deeply." New Testament verses echo this: "The Spirit searches all things, yes, the deep things of God" (1 Corinthians 2:10).

The Spirit also alerts us to sin in our hearts. When Jesus spoke about "the depths of Satan" (Revelation 2:24) He was speaking of the profound deepness of sin, that evil goes down deep into the soul and its roots go down into hell. David said of the wicked: "Both the inward thought and the heart of man are deep" (Psalm 64:6).

These passages all are holy warnings to us. They say, "You do not realize how deeply any association with evil affects you. If you stay on the path of sin you will plummet into the depths of Satan himself, depths that are mysterious, bottomless and profound. This path leads to hell!" Yet in these last days sin has been disguised by complexity, subtlety and sophistication. It comes masked in the guise of art, culture and education. Scripture warns: "Woe to those who seek deep to hide their counsel far from the Lord, and their works are in the dark" (Isaiah 29:15).

The perfect heart wants the Holy Spirit to come and search out the innermost man, to shine into all hidden parts—to investigate, expose and dig out all that is unlike Christ. Those who hide a secret sin, however, do not want to be convicted, searched or probed.

A man once came to me, weeping, during a prayer meeting at Times Square Church. He had left the church a few months before because he thought the messages coming from our pulpit were too piercing. Up to that point, he had been going on with the Lord and growing in spite of himself. But then he left and went to a church where a smooth word was preached. It was not long before he backslid into his old sins. He went through all the motions at that church, and others told him that all was well with his life. Yet he knew better: He knew he was going down deeper into his old sins! Now, at the prayer meeting, he was coming back for the cleansing, unfiltered word of God.

That same night, sitting right next to this man was a man in a wheelchair. He and his wife had come many miles simply because they wanted to hear a convicting word. The man hungered to have his innermost being shaken by God. He told me, "It's been so long since I've heard a message that convicted me." He wanted his heart searched and tried because he wanted a perfect heart.

The ritual of the Old Testament tent-tabernacle provides a clear example of the kind of walk with God the Church should have. The tabernacle had an outer court where the sacrificial animal was slain. This provided the blood covering for sin. But there, as well, was a laver, or basin, in which cleansing took place. No priest could enter the inner court, the Holy of Holies, and commune with God face to face until he was first cleansed.

Yet the modern gospel of today says, "Just go to the altar and, by faith, trust in the blood shed there. Then go boldly into the Holy of Holies. Your Daddy loves you and He is waiting for you. He sees only Jesus in you. You don't need to search your heart. Your sin is under the covering of the blood. All this digging and searching out of sin only brings condemnation and guilt."

Christians who embrace this thinking believe they can bypass the laver, the washing we all need by the water of the Word. They believe they can rush past personal commitment to Him in the holy place, their hearts caked with sin and clinging to sinful habits, then walk right in and boast, "I am the righteousness of God in Christ." They want nothing more than to be covered—a quick ticket to glory. They want no pain, no cross, no cleansing, and they go around crying, "I'm under the blood, I'm safe!"

Those who feel this way take this verse as their authorization: "The blood of Jesus Christ His Son cleanses us from all sin" (1 John 1:7). This statement, however, is only the conclusion of the idea that John is presenting. Here is the rest of it: "If we say that we have fellowship with Him, and walk in darkness, we lie and do not practice the truth. But if we walk in the light as He is in the light . . . the blood of Jesus Christ His Son cleanses us from all sin" (1 John 1:6–7). We must walk in the light if we expect to be cleansed from sin. Jesus said, "Now ye are clean through the word which I have spoken unto you" (John 15:3, KJV). And He was not talking to the world, but to the Church. In Revelation 2:23, Jesus said, "All the churches shall know that I am He who searches the minds and hearts. And I will give to each one of you according to your works."

We must not be deceived: The perfect heart yearns for more than security or a covering for sin. It seeks to be in God's presence always, to dwell in communion. Communion means talking with the Lord, sharing sweet fellowship with Him, seeking His face and knowing His presence. And that is what we get in the Holy of Holies. Our approach to God must come in this order: covering, cleansing, commitment, communion.

The Lord's heart-searchings are not vindictive, but redemptive. His purpose is not to catch us in sin or condemn us, but rather to prepare us to come into His holy presence as clean, pure vessels. "Who may stand in His holy place? He who has clean hands and a pure heart. . . . He shall receive blessing from the Lord" (Psalm 24:3–5).

2. A perfect heart is trusting.

The psalmist wrote, "Our fathers trusted in You; they trusted, and You delivered them. They cried to You, and were delivered; they trusted in You, and were not ashamed" (Psalm 22:4–5). Over and over David testified, "In the Lord I put my trust" (Psalm 11:1), and, "O my God, I trust in You" (25:2).

The Hebrew root word for *trust* suggests "to fling oneself off a precipice." That means being like a child who has climbed up into the rafters and cannot get down. He hears his father say, "Jump!" and he obeys, throwing himself into his father's arms. Are you in such a place right now? Are you on the edge, teetering, and have no other option but to fling yourself into the arms of Jesus? You may have simply resigned yourself to your situation, but that is not trust; it is nothing more than fatalism. Trust is something vastly different from passive resignation. It is *active belief!*

As we hunger for Jesus more intensely, we will find that our trust in Him is well founded. At some point in our lives we may have thought that we could not really trust Him—that He did not really have control over the big picture and that we had to stay in charge. But growing closer to Him and getting to know Him better changes that. It means that we do not just come to Him for help when we are at the end of our rope; instead, we begin to walk with Him so closely that we hear Him warning of the trials ahead.

Think of it this way: In the past we may have pictured the Lord as the captain of some kind of cosmic fire-and-rescue company. It was as if Satan had set the house on fire and we were stranded on the roof yelling, "Lord, help! Save me!" So along came the Lord, with His angels holding a big net, and He said, "Jump." We did jump, the house burned down, and we said, "Thank You, Lord, for getting me out."

Many of us have probably limited our trust at some time to this type of spiritual rescue operation. It is like saying to the Lord, "I trust You to come and put out all my fires—to save me from all my troubles and deliver me out of all my trials. I know You'll be there, Lord, when I need You." In saying this, we think our faith is stretched and that it pleases God. But we do not realize that we have merely credited the devil with being the causer and made the Lord the reactor. We say emphatically, "The devil is behind it!" Yet this viewpoint makes God look as if He only reacts to all the devil's well-laid plans. But our God never reacts—He initiates!

If you have a true walk with Christ you are not the devil's punching bag. He does not have free access to harass or touch you. What kind of father would I be if I allowed a drug pusher, bully or child molester to have free access to any of my children? Yet we go around saying, "The devil did this to me. He shut this door . . . he put this or that on me." I ask you, where do we think our Father is? Sleeping? Doesn't He care about us? Can we really think that He allows us to remain as open prey to rapists and killers? Never! Remember that Satan could not touch Job without God's permission. God had to lower the wall around Job in order for Satan to get to him. Scripture also says Jesus was "led up by the Spirit . . . to be tempted by the devil" (Matthew 4:1). Our God is always in control. Not for one moment has Satan ever been—or will he ever be—beyond the power of God's Word.

A messenger of Satan came to buffet Paul—but only because God allowed it. The Lord would not allow His servant to be lifted up in pride because of the great revelation he had received; God would remain in control. At the same time it is true that at least twice Paul tried to go to Thessalonica, "but Satan hindered" (1 Thessalonians 2:18). Yet the devil could not stop God's work: The believers in Thessalonica later became Paul's "crown of rejoicing."

Likewise, God may allow the devil to have access to our lives for any number of reasons; our own sin or disobedience may lead us to the devil's doorstep when God has been trying to warn us that we are in danger. But His desire is always that we learn to trust in Him, His perfect goodness and lovingkindness. He may allow us to have some hard lessons in order for us to see Him as He really is.

The trusting heart always says, "All my steps are ordered by the Lord. He is my loving Father, and He permits my sufferings, temptations and trials—but never more than I can bear, for He always makes a way of escape. He has an eternal plan and purpose for me. He has numbered every hair on my head, and He formed all my parts when I was in my mother's womb. He knows when I sit, stand or lie down because I am the apple of His eye. He is Lord—not just over *me*, but over every event and situation that *touches* me."

3. A perfect heart is broken.

I once thought I knew what a broken heart was. I felt I had experienced much brokenness until the Holy Spirit opened my eyes to its deeper meaning. As David said, "The Lord is near to those who have a broken heart, and saves such as have a contrite [crushed] spirit" (Psalm 34:18). He also said, "The sacrifices of God are a broken spirit, a broken and a contrite heart—these, O God, You will not despise" (Psalm 51:17).

Brokenness means more than sorrow and weeping, more than a crushed spirit, more than humility. Indeed, many who weep are not brokenhearted. Many who lie before God and groan are not broken in spirit. True brokenness releases in the heart the greatest power God can entrust to mankind—greater than power to raise the dead or heal sickness and disease. When we are truly broken before God, we are given a power that restores ruins, a power that brings a special kind of glory and honor to our Lord.

You see, brokenness has to do with walls—broken-down, crumbling walls. David associated the crumbling walls of Jerusalem with the brokenheartedness of God's people: "The sacrifices of God are a broken spirit, a broken and a contrite heart. . . . Do good in Your good pleasure to Zion; build the walls of Jerusalem. Then You shall be pleased with the sacrifices of righteousness" (Psalm 51:17–19).

Nehemiah was a truly brokenhearted man, and his example has to do with those broken walls of Jerusalem. During the Babylonian exile Nehemiah served as cupbearer to the king. It was in the Babylonian palace at Shushan that he learned the walls of Jerusalem had been torn down and the gates burned. Soon he returned and saw the brokenness for himself:

> I arose in the night, I and a few men with me; I told no one what my God had put in my heart to do at Jerusalem; nor was there any animal with me, except the one on which I rode. . . . I went up in the night by the valley, and viewed the wall; then I turned back and entered by the Valley Gate, and so returned.
>
> Nehemiah 2:12, 15

In the dark of night, Nehemiah "viewed the wall." The Hebrew word *shabar* is used here. It is the same word used in Psalm 51:17 for "broken heart." Some might think Nehemiah's brokenness came when he "sat down and wept, and mourned certain days, and fasted, and prayed before the God of heaven" (Nehemiah 1:4, KJV) when he first heard about the destruction of the walls back in Shushan. Yet his weeping and confessing were only the *beginning* of the breaking. Nehemiah could have stayed in the king's court at the palace, weeping, mourning, fasting for days, confessing and praying. Yet still he would not have had a broken heart. His heart was not fully broken until he came to Jerusalem, saw the ruin and decided to do something about it.

In the fullest Hebrew meaning, Nehemiah's heart was breaking in two ways. It broke first with anguish for the ruin (sharing God's grief as we discussed earlier), and second with a hope for rebuilding (bursting with hope).

This is a truly broken heart: one that first sees the Church and families in ruin and feels the Lord's anguish. Such a heart grieves over the reproach cast on the Lord's name. It also looks deep inside and sees, as David did, its own shame and failure. It cries out, "Lord, I've made a breach in the wall! I've disregarded Your holy testimony. I am crushed by my sins. This cannot go on." But there is a second important element to this brokenness, and that is hope. The truly broken heart has heard from God: "I will heal, restore and build. Get rid of the rubbish, and get to work rebuilding the breaches!"

Several years ago, as I walked through Times Square, I wept and mourned because of all the sin I saw. I went back to my home in Texas, and for more than a year I grieved before the Lord. Then God said, *Go and do something about all the ruin.* I had seen the destruction and been broken over it, but I was not fully broken until I was moved with hope to begin rebuilding the wall—in this case, by coming to New York City to help raise up a church.

Have you been "viewing the ruin" in your own life? Like David, have you sinned and brought reproach on His name? Is there a breach in your wall, something that is not repaired? It is good to fall on the Rock, Jesus, and to be broken into little pieces (see Matthew 21:44). For when we see Christ coming in all His glory, the sight of Him at that time will indeed shatter us. Even the good things in us—talent, efficiency, abilities—will crumble when we stand or fall down before Him, helpless and drained. Like Daniel, who saw the great vision by the river, we will say, "There remained no strength in me: for my comeliness [natural color] was turned in me into corruption [a deathly pallor], and I retained no strength" (Daniel 10:8, KJV).

Brokenness is the total shattering of all human strength and ability. It is the recognition of the full reality of sin and the reproach it brings on Christ. Yet brokenness also means recognizing and heeding the next step: "Stand upright, for I have now been sent to you" (Daniel 10:11). It is the absolute assurance that things are going to change, that healing and rebuilding will come—that our ruins are going to be reclaimed for God! A holy faith says, "God

is at work in me. Satan cannot hold me. I am not going to deterio-
rate or be destroyed. My sin has grieved me, but I have repented.
Now it's time to rise and rebuild." Until we take hold of that hope,
zeal and determination, we will not move past our tears.

Our lives may still appear to be something of a rubble heap. But
if our hearts are open and being searched by God; if we are trusting
that He is sovereignly at work; if we are broken in grief and in hope,
then we possess the most valuable tool for the work of the Kingdom
of God: a perfect heart. We will know communion with God. We
will have His assurance and hope. And we will be His repairer of
breaches in the Body of Christ.

5

WALKING IN HOLINESS

One of the great tragedies of the Church in this generation, and one of God's greatest griefs, is that so many Christians are not truly happy. They put on a good front—singing, clapping, smiling and praising. But lurking just beneath the surface is loneliness and deep misery; their joy does not last.

These Christians are hot, then suddenly cold. They cannot cope with fear. Depression runs over them like a steamroller. One week they are high, the next week low. Many times their marriages follow that pattern as well. One day all is well between a husband and wife, and the next day they are miserable. Some days they cannot even talk to one another. They explain, "Well, that's just the way marriage is supposed to be. You can't expect to stay happy and loving *all* the time."

Believers caught in this up-and-down cycle should heed the words of Paul to Timothy. He encouraged the young man to help others come to their senses and "escape the snare of the devil, having been taken captive by him to do his will" (2 Timothy 2:26), or as the King James Version puts it, "taken captive by him *at his* will." This describes many believers perfectly: Because they give him access, Satan moves in and out of their lives at his own will. They exercise no authority to stop the devil at their heart's door, and he flaunts his hold over them. "You have no power of Christ in you to stop me," he says. "You are my captive and will do as I wish."

This lack of victory in Christ is appalling! Satan places fear, loneliness, depression or lust upon these people at any time he chooses. Is this what Christ died for? To raise up children who are under the power of the devil's will? Is this our testimony to the world: "Give your heart to Jesus, but leave your will to the devil"? Certainly not! There is no reason for a Christian to live as a slave to the devil.

Those who are caught in this satanic snare may blame their unhappiness on suffering, poor health, being misunderstood or having an uncaring mate, boss or friend. They can blame anything they choose, but Paul said the real reason is because they are "in opposition" (see 2 Timothy 2:25). To be in opposition, or "oppose yourself" as the King James Version puts it, means to set oneself up to be trapped, to refuse God's way of deliverance and victory. Such people have opposed His way and set up their own way, and they will not do what must be done to be delivered from the devil's trap.

Are you in this situation? If Satan plays on your emotions and you are getting worse, not better; if your problems are getting bigger; if fear is rising, joy is dissipating and sadness is setting in, then something very serious is wrong. You are a captive to the enemy of your soul. You must recognize the trap you are in and seek to be released. If you have been serving the Lord for more than a few months, you should be growing daily in the grace and knowledge of Jesus. Your spiritual victories should be sweet. You should be assured of His constant presence, and you should be changing from glory to glory into His likeness. By now Satan should be running from *you!*

So what is the problem? Why have so many Christians become captives? It is because their hunger for Christ does not bring them to the point of desiring to walk with Him. They do not seek His holiness. Let's look at the life of a man who lived this to a degree that few have emulated: Enoch. All of us can learn from his example.

Walking with God

"Enoch walked with God" (Genesis 5:24). The original Hebrew meaning for *walked* implies that Enoch went up and down, in and out, to and fro, arm in arm with God, continually conversing with Him and growing closer to Him. Enoch's father, Jared, lived to be 962 years old and Enoch's son Methuselah lived to be 969. Enoch lived 365 years—or, a "year" of years. In him we see a new kind of believer. For 365 days each year for *all* of his 365 years, he walked arm in arm with the Lord. The Lord was his very life—so much so that at the end of his life, he did not see death:

> By faith Enoch was translated that he should not see death; and was not found, because God had translated him: for before his translation he had this testimony, that he pleased God. But without faith it is impossible to please him: for he that cometh to God must believe that he is, and that he is a rewarder of them that diligently seek him.
>
> Hebrews 11:5–6, KJV

Like Enoch, who was translated out of life, those who walk closely with God are translated out of Satan's reach—taken out of his kingdom of darkness and put into Christ's Kingdom of light: "Who hath delivered us from the power of darkness, and hath translated us into the kingdom of his dear Son" (Colossians 1:13, KJV). Right now we stand translated out of the devil's snare and into the very heart of Jesus. The Greek word for *translated* here suggests that Christ comes personally and carries us away from the devil's power and sets us in a heavenly place. God translates only those who walk intimately with Him, like Enoch. Those who are held captive at Satan's will cannot be taken up and delivered from darkness.

I believe that we are not truly saved until we set our hearts firmly on walking with God. We can claim to be saved and to love Him, and we can tell the world we belong to Him. We may even pray, weep and devour His Word. But unless we walk closely with Him every day we will never change. We will fall deeper and deeper into bondage.

Enoch learned to walk pleasingly before God in the midst of a wicked society. Yet he was an ordinary man with all the same problems and burdens we carry. He was not a hermit hidden away in a wilderness cave; he was involved in life with a wife, children, obligations and responsibilities. Enoch wasn't "hiding to be holy."

Today, however, many Christians are running for the hills to hide from the mounting calamities. So-called prophets are telling people to come to their safe rural havens. Messianic Christians are being warned to flee to Israel to escape the financial collapse anticipated in America. But Enoch proved that the greater testimony is to walk with God in the midst of the storm, no matter what. Jesus' command was "Go ye!"—not "Hide ye!"

Yet Enoch knew full well this world was ungodly. He looked down through history to the very last days, and all he could say was, "Ungodly!"

> Now Enoch, the seventh from Adam, prophesied about these men also, saying, "Behold, the Lord comes with ten thousands of His saints, to execute judgment on all, to convict all who are ungodly among them of all their ungodly deeds which they have committed in an ungodly way, and of all the harsh things which ungodly sinners have spoken against Him."
>
> Jude 14–15

We must not hide from the world. But, at the same time, if we are walking with the Lord, then we must also see the world as Enoch saw it—ungodly, full of the spirit of the Antichrist and polluted with harsh speech against our God.

How can we hunger for Jesus and remain part of what is ungodly? How can we desire Him above all else and yet count our-selves with those He is coming to judge? I am not talking here about ministering to a lost world, which is our duty as disciples of Christ. I mean that we cannot be a *part* of that world. I am also not condemning the beauty of nature and the good things God has created. We should "consider the lilies of the field" (Matthew 6:28). But if we are walking arm in arm with Jesus, talking with Him and listening to Him, we will hate this ungodly world system. We will take His side against those who talk against Him. We will heed His Word that "whoever . . . wants to be a friend of the world makes himself an enemy of God" (James 4:4). And when the Lord is coming with tens of thousands of His saints to judge a sinful, lost world, then we will not stand before Him guilty and ashamed.

One other prophet was literally translated, like Enoch, and that was Elijah. The two had something in common: Both hated sin and cried out against it. Both walked so closely with God that they could not help sharing His hatred for ungodliness. This is the undeniable effect on all who hunger totally for God. And not only do they hate it, but they separate themselves from it as well. If we still love this world and are at home with the ungodly, if we are friends with those who curse the Lord, then we are not walking with God and our salvation is a sham. We are sitting on the fence, putting Him to open shame.

"Enoch walked with God; and he was not, for God took him" (Genesis 5:24). We know from Hebrews that this verse speaks of Enoch's translation, the fact that he did not taste death. But it also means something deeper. The phrase *he was not*, as used in Genesis 5, also means "he was not of this world." In his spirit and in his senses, Enoch was not a part of this wicked world. Each day as he walked with the Lord he became less attached to the things below. Day by day, year by year, he was going up, heading home, getting closer to glory. Like Paul, he died daily to this earthly life. And he was taken up in his spirit to a heavenly realm.

Yet while he walked on this earth, Enoch undertook all his responsibilities. He cared for his family; he worked, ministered and occupied. But "he was not"—not earthbound. None of the demands of this life could keep him from his walk with God. The Lord consumed Him; in every waking moment his mind came back to Him. His heart was attached to God with what seemed like a huge rubber band—and the more you stretch a rubber band, the more strongly it springs back when you let it go. Enoch's heart always "sprang back" to the Lord!

Changing into the Lord's Image

All around Enoch mankind grew increasingly ungodly. Yet as men changed into wild beasts full of lust, hardness and sensuality, Enoch became more and more like the One with whom he walked. Likewise you and I are changing and by now, along with many Christians, we should be becoming like Jesus.

This is not true of all believers by any means. Instead many have become hard and selfish. They should be growing in grace, completely satisfied in Him, but they are backsliding and reverting to their old fleshly ways. Why? Because they do not walk with God. They seldom pray. They rarely dig into God's Word. They brood and get hard over life; they pout and open themselves up to the devil's will. They simply do not love Jesus enough to want to be with Him.

As we saw earlier, Hebrews 11:5 says clearly: "Before he was taken [Enoch] had this testimony, that he pleased God." What was it about Enoch that pleased God so much? It was that his walk with God produced in Him the kind of faith God loves. These two verses cannot be separated: "Before his translation he had this testimony, that he pleased God. But without faith it is impossible to please him" (Hebrews 11:5–6). We hear this latter verse often, but rarely in connection with the former. Yet throughout the Bible and all of history those who walked closely with God became men and women of deep faith. If the Church is walking with God daily, communing with Him continually, the result will be a people full of faith—*true faith* that pleases God.

Too many Christians rush to faith seminars, distribute faith tapes and quote "faith Scriptures" all in an effort to produce faith. It is true, "Faith comes by hearing, and hearing by the word of God" (Romans 10:17). But these Christians fail to realize that Jesus *is* the Word. "The letter kills," Scripture says. Without intimacy with Jesus, a Christian who adheres to the letter produces in himself a dead, selfish, demanding emotion that is not faith at all. And God hates it. Faith comes by hearing His Word *and* walking closely with Him; talking without walking will get us nowhere. We should always be "looking unto Jesus, the *author and finisher* of our faith" (Hebrews 12:2).

Faith really consists of knowing who God is. It consists of becoming familiar with His glory and majesty—because those who know Him best trust Him most. Show me a people who walk closely with Him—who actively hate sin, have become detached from this world and are coming to know His voice—and I'll show you a people who won't need much preaching and teaching about faith. They won't need "ten steps" on what faith is and how to get it—because true faith comes out of the very heart of Jesus. And it will be *His* own faith, not theirs, that grows and emerges from their hearts.

"By faith Enoch was translated." This is an incredible truth, almost beyond our comprehension. All of Enoch's faith was focused on the one great desire of his heart: to be with the Lord. And God translated him in answer to his faith. Enoch could no longer bear to stand behind the veil; he just *had* to see the Lord. He prayed, believing that God would answer his cry to be in His actual presence. He so hated the world he experienced on earth that he said to God, "Come, Lord—there's nothing left for me here."

Think of how most Christians squander what they call faith. Theirs is all centered on self—their own needs, their own wants. Where are the Enochs of today, who spend their faith believing to be translated out of the devil's darkness and into the hands of God's dear Son?

Our brother Enoch had no Bible, no songbook, no fellow members, no teachers, no indwelling Holy Spirit, no rent veil with access to the Holy of Holies. *But He knew God!* With neither the reproof of a prophet nor the example of others, Enoch set his heart to follow the Lord. Why is it hard for so many today, with all the available helps, convictions, prophetic warnings and pleadings of the Holy Ghost, to walk in victory? Is it not a rebuke to us that Enoch rose above his wicked day, a man who walked with God despite so little help?

God as Rewarder

"He who comes to God must believe that He is, and that He is a rewarder of those who diligently seek Him" (Hebrews 11:6). How do we know Enoch believed God was a rewarder? Because we know that that is the only faith that pleases God—and we know that Enoch pleased Him! God is a recompenser, a remunerator, that is, One who pays well for faithfulness. How does the Lord reward His diligent ones? I know that when I walk arm-in-arm with Jesus, in love with Him, rewards break out on all sides. Those are times when everything I do or have is blessed: my wife, children, friends and ministry. I see a life of Christ growing within me that flows like a mighty river. Yes, I have trials and tribulations, even in the closest times of walking with Him. But through it all He rewards me with manifestations of His presence.

There are three important rewards that come by believing God and walking with Him in faith.

1. The first reward is God's control of our lives.

The person who neglects the Lord soon spins out of control as the devil moves in and takes over. Such a person has a devastated self-image. His feelings of self-doubt and despair cannot be curbed, and his tongue wags and moves under the power of bitterness and anger. If only he would fall in love with Jesus, walking and talking with Him! God would soon show him that Satan has no real dominion over him and this person would quickly allow Christ to control him. Then he would be chasing demons, putting thousands to flight, standing up by faith against every fear, lie and doubt that comes at him from hell.

2. The second reward that comes by faith is having "pure light."

When we walk with the Lord, we are rewarded with light, direction, discernment, revelation—a certain "knowing" that God gives us. Zacharias prophesied that Christ came "to give light to those who sit in darkness . . . to guide our feet" (Luke 1:79). And as we die to this world day by day, that light grows brighter within us.

When we are truly in love with Jesus, He turns up the light. In His presence there is no darkness at all. But we can deceive ourselves into thinking that we have the true light, when really we have a counterfeit. Jesus warned, "Take heed that the light which is in you is not darkness" (Luke 11:35). Jesus told the Pharisees that judgment falls upon those who pervert or refuse the light:

> "For judgment I have come into this world, that . . . those who see may be made blind." Then some of the Pharisees . . . said to Him, "Are we blind also?" Jesus said to them . . . "Now you say, 'We see.' Therefore your sin remains."
>
> John 9:39–41

Like the Pharisees, some Christians think they "see." They think they have discernment and are in the light. Yet they should look at their lives and homes, at all the trouble and confusion in their hearts and admit, "Lord, I *don't* see. Show me! Am I blind?" If we will not admit to our darkness and open up to true, pure light, then our discernment can only be a false light. The one who goes around saying "I see" is cursed with the worst form of darkness and pride.

Check your heart: Are you under the spell of some kind of darkness or indecision? Are you confused, befuddled or foggy? Then you are still walking in darkness.

Here is your answer: "I am the light of the world. He who follows Me shall not walk in darkness, but have the light of life" (John 8:12). "Whoever believes in Me should not abide in darkness" (John 12:46). "He has delivered us from the power of darkness and conveyed us into the kingdom of the Son of His love" (Colossians 1:13). Go back to walking with Jesus, and He will expose all darkness and restore to you His pure light.

3. The third reward that comes with a walk of faith is protection from all our enemies.

"No weapon formed against you shall prosper" (Isaiah 54:17). In the original Hebrew this verse is translated as: "No plan, no instrument of destruction, no satanic artillery shall push you or run over you, but it will be done away with."

Everything Satan tries in order to get us down just will not work. Those big guns aimed at us will melt away in Christ's presence. Do you think Satan would dare aim at Jesus, with whom we are walking? If he should try, God has promised to wreck his attack upon us.

God said through Isaiah, "I have created the waster to destroy" (Isaiah 54:16, KJV). Remember, "the waster" is under the Lord's control. And the reward of those who diligently seek Him is the privilege of becoming more than conquerers (Romans 8:37) even in the midst of trials and temptations.

For 365 years Enoch shook off every fiery dart. He lived in total victory until his last breath. He did not crawl out, nor did he limp out; he went out in a blaze of life and glory. And God's word to us is the same today:

"In righteousness you shall be established; you shall be far from oppression, for you shall not fear; and from terror, for it shall not come near you. Indeed they shall surely assemble, but not because of Me. Whoever assembles against you shall fall for your sake."

Isaiah 54:14–15

When we walk in holiness, we will be delivered from all oppression. We will not fear, for our security and peace will be in Jesus' righteousness.

Such a basking in His presence will help us see what He has there for us: Hungering for Jesus allows us to take our seats at the King's table. A great revelation awaits us.

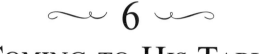

6

Coming to His Table

An old gospel song has profound meaning for me. It says, "Jesus has a table spread / Where the saints of God are fed / He invites His chosen people, come and dine."

What an exciting prospect: The Lord has spread a table in the heavenlies for His followers! Jesus told His disciples, "I bestow upon you a kingdom, just as My Father bestowed one upon Me, that you may eat and drink at My table in My kingdom" (Luke 22:29–30). Hungering for Him means that, by faith, we also are seated at this table. Paul says we have been "raised . . . up . . . and [made to] sit together in the heavenly places in Christ Jesus" (Ephesians 2:6).

We now share the company of Moses, Aaron, Nadab, Abihu and the seventy elders of Israel who ate at the Lord's table on Mount Sinai:

They saw the God of Israel. And there was under His feet as it were a paved work of sapphire stone, and it was like the very heavens in its clarity. But on the nobles of the children of Israel He did not lay His hand. So they saw God, and they ate and drank.

Exodus 24:10–11

What an awesome picture: 74 men of God, seated with Him and eating and drinking at a supernatural table! What a revelation of glory this must have been!

A royal table also was maintained by the kings of Israel, and it was a great honor to be assigned a seat at this table. It was there the king shared his wisdom in glorious intimacy, opening his heart to all who were seated with him. Israel's first three kings give us varied examples.

King Saul assigned a seat at his table to David, but eventually it became a great risk for David to sit there because of Saul's jealousy. In order to test the king's intentions, David and Jonathan, Saul's son, devised a plan to leave David's seat empty and gauge the king's reactions. As expected Saul asked, "Why has the son of Jesse not come to eat, either yesterday or today?" (1 Samuel 20:27). When Jonathan said that David had gone to visit his family, Saul flew into a rage and revealed his intention to kill him.

Later David, as king, granted a seat at his table to Jonathan's son Mephibosheth: "Do not fear, for I will surely show you kindness for Jonathan your father's sake . . . and you shall eat bread at my table continually" (2 Samuel 9:7).

In King Solomon's day the Queen of Sheba marveled at the glorious feast of the royal table. She was breathless as she beheld "the food on his table, the seating of his servants, the service of his waiters and their apparel, his cupbearers and their apparel" (2 Chronicles 9:4). When she saw and heard what took place at that table, she exclaimed: "Happy are your men and happy are these your servants, who stand continually before you and hear your wisdom!" (2 Chronicles 9:7).

Can you see the spiritual significance of this? In the Old Testament, the table of kings represented feasting with the King of kings at His heavenly table!

When the apostle Paul instructs, "Let us keep the feast" (1 Corinthians 5:8), he means let us understand clearly that we have been assigned a seat in the heavenlies with Christ at His royal table. Paul is saying, "Always show up. Never let it be said your seat is empty."

If Saul could say of David, "Why does he not come to my table? Where is he?," cannot our Lord say the same of us, who have no justification for missing a feast? He says, "I gave you an assigned seat at My royal table. This is where My servants see My face, hear My wisdom and get to know Me. It is where I feed them the Bread of Life and it is a great honor. Why then do you take it so lightly? Why do you not take your seat? You run about working for Me and speaking of Me—but why do you not sit with Me and learn of Me? Where have you been?"

The sad truth is that the Church of Jesus Christ simply does not comprehend what it means to keep the feast. We do not understand the majesty and honor accorded us by having been raised by Christ to sit with Him in heavenly places. We have become too busy to sit at His table. We mistakenly derive our spiritual joy from service instead of from communion. We do more and more for a Lord whom we know less and less. We run ourselves ragged giving our bodies and minds to His work, but we seldom keep the feast. And because we miss the feast so often, our generation has a stilted, stunted vision of the Lord Jesus Christ. In spite of all our preaching, praise and endless talk about Him, few Christians really know Him.

Picture the Lord looking down upon the earth, watching the multitudes of those who call themselves by His name—pastors, missionaries, Christian workers, saints of God. What is it that the Lord wants most of all from those who claim to be devoted to Him? What blesses, pleases and delights Him most? To build Him something? To start more churches? more Bible schools? more evangelistic centers? more homes and institutions for hurting people? No, He who dwells "not in buildings made by hands" wants much more than that. Solomon thought he had built an everlasting Temple for God, but within fifty years it was in decay. In fewer than four hundred years, it was gone completely. In light of eternity, that is four winks of the eye. What can we possibly accomplish for God's glory when He already *has* all the glory?

The one thing our Lord seeks above all else from His servants, ministers and shepherds is communion at His table. This table is a place for spiritual intimacy, and it is spread daily. Keeping the feast means coming to Him continually for food, strength, wisdom and fellowship.

In Galatians, Paul speaks of the three years after his conversion that he spent separated with God in the desert of Arabia and in Damascus (1:17–18). Those three years were glorious for Paul because he spent them sitting in the heavenlies at the table of the Lord. It was there Christ taught the apostle all he knew, and the wisdom of God was manifested to him.

Indeed, for Paul, conversion was not enough. Nor was a one-time, blinding vision of Christ, a miraculous hearing of His voice from heaven. In spite of having had one of the most direct spiritual calls a man of God has ever received, Paul wanted yet more. Something in his soul cried out, "Oh, that I might know Him!" (see Philippians 3:10).

No wonder Paul could say to the entire Christian Church, "I determined not to know anything among you except Jesus Christ and Him crucified" (1 Corinthians 2:2). He was saying, "Let the Judaizers keep their legalism. Let the Sabbatarians argue their points of doctrine. Let those who seek to be justified by works wear themselves out. Let everyone else think he is passing me by with all his worldly wisdom. As for me, I will know nothing but Jesus Christ."

In order to keep the feast we need three things.

1. We need a revelation of the vastness of Christ.

Ever since the cross, all spiritual giants have had one thing in common: They revered the table of the Lord. They became lost in the glorious vastness of Christ. They all died lamenting that they still knew so little of Him and His life. So it was with Paul, the disciples and many early Church fathers; with Luther, Zwingli and the Puritans; with the pious English and Irish preachers over the past two centuries, men such as Wesley, Whitefield, Fletcher, Müller, Stoney, Mackintosh, Austin-Sparks. And so it has been with the pious American church leaders, such as Tozer, Ravenhill and many others.

This is a powerful roll call of men, and every one of them shared the same ruling passion: an ever-increasing revelation of Jesus Christ. They cared nothing for success, ambition, worldly fame or the spectacular. They prayed not for things, not for blessings, not to be used of God, not for anything of self, but rather only for a fuller revelation of the glory and vastness of their Lord.

With the devil on the loose, displaying great wrath because he knows his time is limited, Christians need exactly this: a greater revelation of Christ. Satan is exerting great power in these last days, and hell is unleashing all its fury. The enemy's strongholds are much more fortified, powerful and deeply entrenched than in any past generation. Without question, Satan—his power, his kingdom and his work—is on the increase. He is becoming better known, less feared and more accepted. And in this final battle against him, a basic Bible school knowledge of Christ will not be enough. In fact, knowing a lot about Christ will not be enough. We need to quit studying Christ, and instead go to His table and let the Holy Spirit *reveal Him* to us. This requires time.

I have read a number of volumes written about Jesus Christ, but found that in many of them the authors really didn't know Him. Their descriptions were clinical, precise and doctrinally pure, but ultimately lifeless. These authors had not been eating and drinking in His presence. Yet that is how we come to know Him—by sitting with Him, hearing His voice and waiting on Him to impart divine wisdom. Busy, preoccupied people never get to know Christ. They live for years on some past vision of glory, with no fresh word or new revelation of Him. They honor and exalt Christ, but He has not become their very life.

You cannot go into battle in this world, where demons rule virtually uncontested, unless you are committed to having an ever-increasing revelation of Christ's power and glory. Otherwise, you will have no impact against the kingdom of darkness. The principalities and powers of evil will scoff at you. Only those who know Christ in fullness and in ever-increasing vision will send fear throughout hell. We must be on our knees often. We must come into the battle directly from the throne room of God. Otherwise we will crumble before the enemy.

Our vision of Christ today is too small, too limited. A gospel of "vastness" is needed to overcome the complicated and growing problems of this wicked age. You see, God does not merely solve problems in this world—He swallows them up in His vastness! Someone with an increasing revelation of Christ's vastness need fear no problem, no devil, no power on this earth. He knows that Christ is bigger than it all. If we had this kind of revelation of how vast He is, how boundless, measureless, limitless and immense, we would never again be overwhelmed by life's problems.

In the past ten years enough "how-to" books on the Christian life have been written to fill the Library of Congress. There is an easy-formula book on every subject known to mankind, each promising relief from problems. Yet little of such advice is of any value, for it is all based on a stunted vision of the vastness of Christ. Because most believers do not genuinely hunger for God; because they do not drink the Word and feed on Christ daily, they become vulnerable to the spirit of the age.

Think of all the troubled marriages among God's people: Decades of advice have failed. Books, cassettes and seminars all have had relatively little effect. In fact, the problems have only grown worse. What we truly need to heal this and every other calamity is to rush back to the Lord's presence, to enter the secret closet of prayer, sit at the Lord's table and become lost in the fullness and vastness of Christ. All of our answers will come from time spent at His table, learning of Him!

Again, Paul is an example to us. He was committed to having such an ever-increasing revelation of Christ. In fact, all he had of Christ came by revelation; it was taught to him at the Lord's table and made truth to him by the Holy Spirit. Remember, it was three years after his conversion before Paul went to spend time with the apostles in Jerusalem, and he stayed with them only fifteen days before continuing his missionary journeys. He later said, "By revelation He made known to me the mystery" (Ephesians 3:3). The

Holy Spirit knows the deep and hidden secrets of God, and Paul prayed constantly for the gift of grace to understand and preach "the unsearchable riches of Christ" (Ephesians 3:8). We have "boldness and access" to these glorious riches, he said, "with confidence through faith in Him" (verse 12).

God, forgive us for not taking advantage of our "access with confidence" to Your vast riches in glory!

The Lord is looking for believers who are not satisfied with sifting through all the conflicting voices to find a true word. He wants us to hunger for a revelation of Him that is all our own—a deep, personal intimacy.

2. We need more intensive preaching.

If you are a preacher, missionary or teacher, think about this: What are you teaching? Is it what a person taught you? Is it a rehashing of the revelation of some great preacher? Or have you experienced your own personal revelation of Jesus Christ? If you have, is it ever-increasing? Is heaven opened to you?

We ministers need to preach Christ with growing intensity.

Paul said, "In Him we live and move and have our being" (Acts 17:28). True men and women of God live within this very small yet vast circle. Their every move, their entire existence, is wrapped up only in the interests of Christ. Years ago I knew the Holy Spirit was drawing me into such a ministry, one that preached Christ alone. Oh, how I yearned to preach nothing but Him! But my heart was divided, and I found the circle too narrow. As a result, I had no flow of revelation to sustain my preaching.

To preach nothing but Christ we must have a continuous flow of revelation from the Holy Spirit. Otherwise, we will end up repeating a stale message. If the Holy Spirit knows the mind of God and searches the deep and hidden things of the Father, and if He is to well up as flowing water within us, then we must be available to be filled with that flowing water. We must stay filled up with a never-ending revelation of Christ. Such revelation awaits every servant of the Lord who is willing to wait on Him, believing and trusting the Holy Spirit to manifest to him the mind of God.

Today we have so little fresh truth, so little of a clear and precious word from the Lord. Our churches are overrun with would-be prophets who claim, "God told me this," or, "I have a word from God for you." Most of this is nonsense! What the Church needs most right now is God's infallible Word—that is, a true and living revelation of it. Multitudes in congregations are trying to sift through all the clamoring voices to hear a clear word from God. They are becoming weary of a barrage of voices, voices, voices. And they are finding only a few kernels of wheat from among the mountains of chaff.

All over the world, God's people are ready to move on in the Lord. They are hungry for more of Jesus and tired of all the lightness and foolishness being preached in the pulpit. And right now the Lord is calling His Bride to come out from among the foolish and the lighthearted. A holy, weeping, praying remnant is arising out of Laodicea. And my concern is, will there be enough servants of God in our pulpits with sufficient anointing and fresh revelation to sustain the sheep? Or will the sheep outgrow their shepherds? Will there be nourishment for all those who are going deeper with the Lord?

I was once a "big-time" evangelist with an entourage of road men and backup people. Thousands came to hear me preach. But I grew steadily empty, having become too busy to receive fresh revelation from Christ. I wept alone often, lonely and hurting. Then, in my desperation, a saint of God gave me a copy of *The Christian in Complete Armour* by William Gurnall, a Puritan writer. The message crushed me with its depth of knowledge of the Lord. I admitted, "I don't know God the way this man does." And that did it—I shut down everything. I pored through the Puritans, the later writers, and on and on—all of those pious men I mentioned earlier. These writers made me hungrier to find my own place in Him. I read them all until God said, *Stop! Now eat* My *Word.*

We must not be deceived: Good works will not dispel emptiness. Preaching on social issues will not either. Those old Spurgeon notes will not take care of it. And the best storytelling in the world will not help. All of our personal experiences and clever life-applications just won't cut it. Nothing will get us in the flow of the revelation knowledge of Jesus Christ until we put up our notes, stop studying other preachers and study Christ alone in the secret closet of prayer. We all serve the same God and we all are taught by the same Holy Spirit, as has been every man and woman who has grown into the fullness of Christ. It simply must become a matter of hunger and desperation. We must become hungry enough to *eat His Book*, to get our own touch of God.

If you have been lax in this area, I encourage you: Determine in your heart to preach Christ next year in fuller measure than you did this year. Stay fresh. Offer Christ alone; go from glory to glory. Away with all success preaching, motivational preaching, self-image preaching, political preaching. They are but dregs peddled by those without a fresh revelation of Christ.

3. We need an increase of Christ's life within.

Once I received a letter from a godly father in Christ. Reading the letter was like hearing from the apostle Paul. He wrote,

> The fact that Paul saw "only in part" did neither lessen the glory of what he did see, nor make it more difficult for him to declare it. I believe that in all our seeking after Him, we have to recognize that it is the *knowledge of Him* we truly need; and the truth we seek is truth that must be wrought out within us by the spirit of life before it actually becomes ours. Knowing this, we begin to understand that God does not see fit to impart more, nor should we desire more, than we are able to digest and build into our lives. Revelation can do us more harm than good if there is not a corresponding ministration of life in our spirit. The Tree of Life is still more desirable than the Tree of Knowledge. Just in knowing and seeing Him we are suddenly growing to know and understand mysteries of truth that we could never unravel in any kind of research. "Working in you that which is well-pleasing in his sight" (Hebrews 13:21, KJV).

This man's message to me echoed the apostle Paul, for he said Christ was being revealed *in* him, not just *to* him (Galatians 1:16). In God's eyes it is a crime to preach a word that has not already worked its power in the preacher's life and ministry. It may seem all right for certain shallow ones to preach Christ with contention—but not so for the man or woman of God. We must preach an ever-increasing revelation of Christ, yet only as that revelation effects a deep change in us. My prayer now is, "O God, let me preach only that which I understand by the Spirit. Let it be a fullness of Christ. Let it first become a part of my nature and character, a part of my own spiritual history with You."

Paul also voiced a personal concern: "Lest . . . when I have preached to others, I myself should be a castaway" (1 Corinthians 9:27, KJV). Paul certainly never would have doubted his security in Christ; that was not in his mind here. The Greek word used for *castaway* means "unapproved" or "not worthy." Paul dreaded the thought of standing before the Judgment Seat of Christ to be judged for preaching a Christ he really did not know or for proclaiming a Gospel he did not fully practice. This is why Paul speaks so often of the "living Christ" or "Christ living in me." In Paul's eyes, any minister who preaches to others must always be increasing in his knowledge *and practice* of Christ, or he is unapproved.

We cannot continue another hour calling ourselves servants of God until we can answer this question personally: *Do I truly want nothing but Christ? Is He truly everything to me, my one purpose for living?*

Is your answer yes? If you mean it, you will be able to point to a dung heap of your life, the one that Paul spoke of in "counting everything worthless that I might win Christ." Have you counted all things as loss for the revelation of Him? If you want nothing but Christ then your ministry is not a career—your ministry is prayer! If He is all-in-all to you, you will refuse as wickedness the ladder of success. You will hide yourself away with Him. You will not have to be prodded to seek Him; you will go often to your secret closet, knowing that the moment you walk in you are seated at His table. You will worship Him, sitting in His presence unhurried, loving Him, praising Him with upraised hands, yearning after Him and thanking Him for His wisdom.

So many of us use Christ to further our own ministries, to build our own kingdoms, to advance our own careers. We trade on His name. God, forgive us! Do we really love Him? Do we truly want only Him? We must settle that question first. Until we know that Christ alone is all we need and desire, we should not go anywhere or do anything in His name, because the only thing we can give to people that will transform them is *what we have of Christ*. And that comes from time spent sitting at His table, feasting on Him alone.

~ 7 ~

TAKING HOLD OF CHRIST

I am convinced that many who call themselves Christians will not be able to endure the end times. The Word proclaims that in the latter days the love of many will grow cold and die because of the explosive power of wickedness. Some will turn away from the truth and follow false teachers and prophets who will deceive them and cater to their selfish lusts. Others will be seduced by doctrines of demons and will become spiritually blind. In the end God will give them over to their reprobate minds.

That having been said, I thank God for the letters I have been receiving from committed Christians across the country. It is clear to me that a hunger for Jesus is growing among His people! I have read wonderful testimonies of how the Spirit of God is compelling earnest, searching believers to embark on a walk of holiness. Their spiritual discernment is increasing greatly. Many are forsaking idols, dead churches and false teachings. Among these are ministers of all denominations who now weep for their sheep and preach with the true burden of the Lord. I marvel at the tremendous changes we are hearing about and seeing, as many write to tell us how the Lord is bringing them through His refining fire. For all this I give the Lord praise.

Yet my heart still grieves because those who are turning wholeheartedly to the Lord represent only a small, despised remnant. The majority of Christians—and even shepherds—are shutting out the sound of the trumpet and ignoring the watchman's cry. The spiritual blindness of the churchgoing masses must be growing intolerable for God, because now we see Him moving quickly and openly in judging His people. The Redeemer has come suddenly to Zion with great indignation, and He will not withdraw His hand of judgment until every last moneychanger and thief has been driven out of His house. We are seeing only the beginning of His awesome judgments upon crookedness, lies, deceptions and evil distortions of His Gospel. The shaking has only begun! "For the time has come for judgment to begin at the house of God; and if it begins with us first, what will be the end of those who do not obey the gospel of God?" (1 Peter 4:17).

The Needs of the Sheep

A pastor once wrote me: "You speak out about the failures of shepherds, but you don't tell us where we are failing. I ask in love that you back it with truth."

The failure lies in this: *We ministers of the Gospel are not holding fast to our purpose of pressing upon believers the true cost of discipleship.* Jesus made stern, uncompromising demands on those who chose to follow Him and confess His holy name.

We see in our pulpits today too much ego and pride and not enough alarm and grief over sin. Few ministers now preach in tears and agony about the backsliding and coldness among believers. It is tragic that so many shepherds have lost the anointing of the Holy Spirit and now devote themselves to building their own reputations. Their eyes focus not on the needs of the sheep, but on financing and promoting their own expensive dreams.

The apostle Paul had a true pastor's heart—one always in travail and always concerned for the spiritual growth of the sheep. He wrote to the Corinthians, "I am jealous for you with godly jealousy. For I have betrothed you to one husband, that I may present you as a chaste virgin to Christ" (2 Corinthians 11:2). He spoke of the Galatian sheep as "my little children, for whom I labor in birth again until Christ is formed in you" (Galatians 4:19). He wrote to the Thessalonians of "night and day praying exceedingly that we may see your face and perfect what is lacking in your faith" (1 Thessalonians 3:10).

My heart breaks when I realize how far short I fall in measuring up to what a loving shepherd ought to be. Often I desperately lack the Spirit that moved Paul with such love and concern for the people of God: "For what is our hope, or joy, or crown of rejoicing? Is it not even you in the presence of our Lord Jesus Christ at His coming? For you are our glory and joy. . . . For now we live, if you stand fast in the Lord" (1 Thessalonians 2:19–20; 3:8). This man of God encouraged the sheep with letters that provoked them to holiness and great hunger for Jesus Christ. With tears he said to them, "We also pray always for you . . . that the name of our Lord Jesus Christ may be glorified in you, and you in Him" (2 Thessalonians 1:11–12). "We were gentle among you, just as a nursing mother cherishes her own children. . . . [We] exhorted, and comforted, and charged every one of you, as a father does his own children" (1 Thessalonians 2:7, 11).

Paul did not want these people's money. He took great care never to be a burden to them. He wrote that he "worked with labor and toil night and day, that we might not be a burden to any of you" (2 Thessalonians 3:8). When he justifiably could have received financial support from them, Paul instead chose to support himself. He refused to put on a "cloak of covetousness" because he had been entrusted with the Gospel. He summed up his goal in ministry in this verse: "So that He may establish your hearts blameless in holiness before our God" (1 Thessalonians 3:13).

I beseech God that He would give me such a loving shepherd's heart! Oh, that the Holy Spirit would raise up pastors and evangelists today who have no goal in ministry other than to establish believers in holiness and to provoke them to lay hold of Christ!

Tragically, those in ministry have so watered down God's truth about self-denial that we have birthed a generation of loose-living, impotent believers who do not understand the meaning of separation from the world. Many of our churches have so mixed worldliness into their messages that Christians can now out-sin the wicked without blushing! In fact, in recent years the world has been shocked and outraged by the filth and corruption in Christendom, and justifiably so.

Much Gospel preaching today contains no mention of the cross, no doctrine of suffering, no reproof, no repentance, no hatred for sin, no demand for separation or purity, no call for unconditional surrender to the Lordship of Christ, no daily death to self, no crucifixion of the fleshly lusts, no self-denial, no rejection of the self-life, no warnings of coming persecution and imminent judgment. And, most tragic of all, many Christians now prefer to hear about their rights in Christ—and ignore *His* claims on *us*!

Christ's Claims on Us

Multitudes followed Jesus, yet He knew only a few would hold fast to Him and become true disciples. The Jews wanted to hold to both Jesus and Moses, to keep their traditions and dead rituals while claiming to be Christ's followers. But Jesus would have nothing to do with their double-mindedness.

"No one can serve two masters; for either he will hate the one and love the other, or else he will be loyal to the one and despise the other. You cannot serve God and mammon" (Matthew 6:24). Jesus exposes here the paradox of a divided heart. He tears away the façade of phony discipleship and shows us the fate of those who try to serve two masters at the same time. We dare not miss our Lord's pointed warning: *Unforsaken sin will lead into the worst hypocrisy possible.* Some say they love the Lord and hate the devil, but by clinging to secret lusts, idolatry, bitterness or rebellion, they instead despise the Lord and hold onto Satan. They secretly give their allegiance to the one they say they hate, while giving only lipservice to loving their God.

To such hypocrites Jesus said, "These people draw near to Me with their mouth, and honor Me with their lips, but their heart is far from Me. . . . In vain they worship Me" (Matthew 15:8–9). He is saying, "No one can testify that I am the One he loves and at the same time despise Me by his evil doings." The Greek meaning of the word *despise* is "to esteem lightly." To despise the Lord is not to take His Word to heart—to disregard His claims as if they are not binding. Let me list just three of the claims Christ has on us as we desire to take hold of Him:

1. He calls His followers to love Him so passionately that all other affections appear as hatred in comparison.

"If anyone comes to Me and does not hate his father and mother, wife and children, brothers and sisters, yes, and his own life also, he cannot be My disciple."

Luke 14:26

The Greek word for *hate* means "to love less by comparison." Jesus is calling us to have a love for Him that is so all-inclusive, fervent and absolute that all our earthly affections cannot come close.

If we had that red-hot, all-consuming, intense and joyous love for Christ, we would not need outlines, diagrams and instructions telling us how to pray; we would pray because our hearts would be on fire with love for Him. We would not grow bored trying to fill up an hour praying ambiguously for needs all over the world; Christ would be the object of our prayers, and our prayer time would be precious. We would spend hours behind closed doors, expressing the overflowing admiration and sweet love that flood our hearts for Him. Reading His Word would never be a burden; we wouldn't need formulas on how to finish the Bible in a year. If we loved Jesus passionately we would be drawn magnetically to His Word to learn more about Him. And we would not become bogged down with endless genealogies and end-time speculations. We would want only to know Him better—to see more of His beauty and glory so that we could become more like Him.

Think about it: Do we know what it is like to come into His sweet presence and ask nothing? To reach out to Him only because we are grateful that He loves us so completely?

We have become selfish and self-centered in our prayers: "Give us . . . meet us . . . help us . . . bless us . . . use us . . . protect us." All this may be scriptural, but the focus remains on us. We go to His Word for answers to our problems, for guidance and comfort, and this also is right and commendable. But where is the love-motivated soul who searches the Scriptures diligently, who wants only to discover more and more about his beloved Lord?

Even our work for the Lord has become selfish. We want Him to bless our service to Him, so we can know our faith is genuine. We want to be considered diligent, capable and successful as a sign of His blessing upon us. I have been crying out in my own heart, "O Lord, is my own ministry more important to me than You? Is love my only motive for my Savior, or do I want to see something tangible that I have accomplished for You?" You see, our Lord is more interested in what we are *becoming in Him* than in what we are *doing for Him.*

Someone reading this may be hurting because doors of ministry have closed. He or she may feel "put on the shelf." Someone else may think he would be more useful to the Lord on some needy mission field. But I say we cannot be more useful to the Lord than when we minister love to Him in the secret closet of prayer. When we seek the Lord, when we search His Word endlessly to know Him, then we are at the peak of our usefulness. We do more to bless and satisfy God by being shut up with Him in loving communication than by doing anything else. Whatever work He might open up for us to do, at home or abroad, will flow effortlessly out of our communion with Him. He is more interested in winning our whole hearts than in our winning the world for Him.

2. He calls us to see it through.

> "Which of you, intending to build a tower, does not sit down first and count the cost, whether he has enough to finish it—lest, after he has laid the foundation, and is not able to finish, all who see it begin to mock him, saying, 'This man began to build and was not able to finish.' "
>
> Luke 14:28–30

Christ knew many of His followers would not have what it took to see them through. He knew they would turn back and not finish the race. I believe this is the most tragic condition possible for a believer—to have started out fully intending to lay hold of Christ, to grow into a mature disciple and become more like Jesus and then to drift away, becoming cold and indifferent to Him. Such a person is the one who laid a foundation and could not finish because he did not first count the cost. He went only so far because he ran out of resources and then quit.

What a joy it is to meet those who are indeed finishing the race! These believers are growing in the wisdom and knowledge of Christ. They are changing daily, from moment to moment. Paul says to them encouragingly, "We all, with unveiled face, beholding as in a mirror the glory of the Lord, are being transformed into the same image from glory to glory, just as by the Spirit of the Lord" (2 Corinthians 3:18). They are becoming increasingly distant from the world and its pleasures. They are becoming heavenly minded, their spiritual senses exercised, their discernment increasing. The older they get, the hungrier they grow for Christ. They break loose from all earthly attachments, and with growing intensity they long to be with Jesus in His glory. For them, to die is gain, because the ultimate prize is to be called into His presence and remain at His side forevermore. It is not heaven these believers seek, but Christ in His glory!

We can be sure that when Jesus returns, He will have a glorious Church consisting of those who have been changed into His likeness. Her members will have become so unattached to this world and so united to Him that moving from the corruptible state to the incorruptible will be just one last step of love. It will be like breaking through a thin veil of tissue, because they will already have drawn so close to Christ in this life.

I know that many who read this particular message are in the process of pausing or taking a step backward. It may seem like a small step, but it will cause a swift decline away from His love. If this is true of you, realize the Holy Spirit is calling you all the way back—back to repentance, self-denial and surrender. And at this very moment, time is a big factor. If you ever intend to lay hold of Christ, do it now; see it through!

3. He calls us to fight Satan.

"What king, going to make war against another king, does not sit down first and consider whether he is able with ten thousand to meet him who comes against him with twenty thousand? Or else, while the other is still a great way off, he sends a delegation and asks conditions of peace. So likewise, whoever of you does not forsake all that he has cannot be My disciple."

Luke 14:31–33

Enoch once prophesied, "Behold, the Lord comes with ten thousands of His saints" (Jude 14). Scripture says we are kings and priests unto the Lord, and we represent these tens of thousands going out to battle Satan's army. Satan wars against us because he hates us greatly: "And the dragon was enraged with the woman, and he went to make war with the rest [the remnant, KJV] of her offspring, who keep the commandments of God and have the testimony of Jesus Christ" (Revelation 12:17). If we have set our hearts to lay hold of Christ, we have become the devil's target in this final conflict. He will hurl everything in hell against us.

We must be prepared for what is coming. We must be ready to spend our days in spiritual warfare, knowing that a flood of iniquity is aimed against the people of God. If we are determined to lay hold of Christ, then we need to realize that we are invincible in Christ.

It is written, "Greater is He that is in you than he that is in the world" (see 1 John 4:4). God says we are guaranteed victory over all the power of the enemy; we have all the hosts of heaven fighting for us!

This is especially encouraging because, as we have noted, the devil is amassing greater power. We do well to remember the words Moses spoke to Israel for God:

> "You shall not make idols for yourselves. . . . Walk in . . . My commandments, and perform them, [and in turn] you will chase your enemies, and they shall fall by the sword before you. Five of you shall chase a hundred, and a hundred of you shall put ten thousand to flight; your enemies shall fall by the sword before you."
>
> Leviticus 26:1, 3, 7–8

Joshua also encouraged the Lord's army with these words: "One man of you shall chase a thousand, for the Lord your God is He who fights for you. . . . Therefore take careful heed to yourselves, that you love the Lord your God" (Joshua 23:10–11).

Moses told them what would happen if they mingled with the world and attempted to serve two masters. "How could one chase a thousand, and two put ten thousand to flight, unless their Rock had sold them, and the Lord had surrendered them?" (Deuteronomy 32:30). Those who no longer cling to the Rock—Christ—become cowardly and fearful before the enemy. Sin and lukewarmness rob them of all power and confidence. They will leave their first love and end up running in fright from the devil's harassment.

If they continue to refuse to let go of secret sin and hidden lusts, these double-minded Christians will eventually try to make a deal with the devil. They will seek conditions of peace by sending their consciences out to meet the enemy and negotiate a truce. They want to continue their claim of loving the Lord, but they don't want to give up that last stronghold, that one besetting sin. And they make this truce with the full knowledge that the devil still rules as the god of this world. He could swallow them up at any time!

We cannot make deals with the devil. We cannot compromise

with sin even slightly. We cannot allow our faith to be shipwrecked by compromise and false peace for even one moment. We are in an all-out war and we have to defeat the enemy *completely* to have victory over all his claims on us.

May God give us more Holy Ghost fight so that each of us can shout to the world and all the hordes of hell, "Nothing shall separate me from the love of Christ! Not tribulation, or distress, or persecution, or famine, or nakedness, or peril, or war. No, in all these things I am more than a conqueror through Him who loves me. For I am persuaded that neither death nor life, nor angels nor principalities nor powers, nor things present nor things to come, nor height nor depth, nor any other created thing, shall be able to separate me from the love of God which is in Christ Jesus our Lord" (see Romans 8:35, 37–39).

This is the battle cry of those who hunger for Jesus.

8

A LETTER FROM THE DEVIL

The Old Testament tells the story of how King Hezekiah of Judah received a letter from the devil:

> And Hezekiah received the letter of the hand of the messengers, and read it: and Hezekiah went up into the house of the Lord . . . and said, O Lord God of Israel, which dwellest between the cherubim, thou art the God, even thou alone, of all the kingdoms of the earth; thou hast made heaven and earth. Lord, bow down thine ear, and hear: open, Lord, thine eyes, and see: and hear the words . . . Sennacherib [has sent] to reproach the living God.
>
> 2 Kings 19:14–16, KJV

The letter that Hezekiah, king of Judah, received was signed by Sennacherib, king of Assyria—but it was sent directly from hell! Sennacherib's name means "man of sin" (also, "moon-god who multiplies brothers"). He represents Satan, the god of this world, who is determined to create for himself a vast brotherhood of God-haters.

At the time Hezekiah received this satanic letter, Jerusalem was under siege by the mighty Assyrian army. King Sennacherib and his hosts had already carried the ten tribes of Israel into captivity. Israel had come under God's judgment for her immorality, idolatry and apostasy. The people had "sold themselves to do evil," and this had been the result:

> For he rent Israel from the house of David. . . . For the children of Israel walked in all the sins of Jeroboam . . . [and] the Lord removed Israel out of his sight. . . . So was Israel carried away out of their own land to Assyria.
>
> 2 Kings 17:21–23, KJV

In this passage, Israel represents the backslidden, sin-saturated, harlot churches of today. Israel was full of compromise, lust, adultery, homosexuality—sheer pleasure-madness. And just as is true today, the Israelites possessed a form of godliness without power: "And the king of Assyria brought men from Babylon . . . and placed them in the cities of Samaria. . . . [T]hey feared not the Lord" (2 Kings 17:24–25, KJV). A gospel of mixture was evident among their ranks—and it went with them into captivity: "So these nations feared the Lord, *and* served their graven images" (2 Kings 17:41, KJV).

Today the devil has no need to seduce, harangue or write threatening letters to such a people. That is because he already controls this segment of the Church! In fact, he has placed his very own "angels of light" in the pulpits. He has entrusted to them a lukewarm religion of mixture: just enough tradition combined with a great deal of wickedness.

No, the devil's onslaught today remains focused on those precious ones whose hearts are set wholly on hungering after the Lord Jesus. In the story of Hezekiah and Sennacherib, the nation of Judah represents the Lord's remnant Church on earth. She is Satan's target because she is under covenant with the Lord and, therefore, poses a tremendous threat to the kingdom of darkness.

Scripture says Judah's King Hezekiah was a godly man:

And he did that which was right in the sight of the Lord. . . . He removed the high places, and brake the images, and cut down the groves. . . . He trusted in the Lord God of Israel; so that after him was none like him among all the kings of Judah, nor any that were before him. For he clave to the Lord, and departed not from following him, but [obeyed] his commandments. . . . And the Lord was with him; and he prospered whithersoever he went forth.

2 Kings 18:3–7, KJV

This is why the "man of sin" was out to destroy Hezekiah. And it is the very same reason Satan will attack you.

"No More Tribute to the Enemy!"

Up to this time Judah had been a servant nation to Assyria, which was a form of bondage. Thus, the man of sin had yet a place in Zion. In events leading up to the delivery of the letter, Assyria's king had taxed Judah three hundred talents of silver and thirty talents of gold.

And Hezekiah gave him all the silver that was found in the house of the Lord, and in the treasures of the king's house. At that time did Hezekiah cut off the gold from the doors of the temple of the Lord.

2 Kings 18:15–16, KJV

This is a picture of compromise and it can be found in God's Church today: Christians walk in fear and intimidation, accommodate worldliness and are afraid to step out boldly and expose sin for what it is. Just as Hezekiah bowed to the desires of the man of sin, the Church today pays tribute to the devil by producing wicked rock and roll music, calling for "Christian" entertainment and practicing double standards.

Yet, in this story, Hezekiah's heart was finally stirred. He cried, "No more tribute to the enemy!" This was a type of Holy Ghost awakening, a calling apart of a holy remnant-people who would no longer compromise or fear the man of sin. At one time, in another crisis, the children of Israel had tried leaning on the arm of flesh by sending for aid from Egypt. But Egypt proved to be no help to them at all. Now, the people of Judah and their leadership cast themselves wholly upon the Lord.

Yet here was the conflict: As long as this people paid tribute to the devil, they remained unmolested. They had no opposition, no war. But then Hezekiah stepped out in faith toward God. He decided there would be no more appeasing the devil, no more halfway discipleship, no more compromise or worldly ties, regardless of the cost. And that's when he received a letter from the devil.

You see, the moment you give up on this world and put your life wholly in the hands of the Lord—watch out: All hell will come against you! You will become a target of the devil, and you will come under siege from the man of sin. You will be tested severely to see if you will really trust God in all things. And everywhere you look, you will see the enemy standing against you.

Satan Uses Subtle Devices Against the Remnant

The Assyrians represent today's "guides to prosperity." The devil will parade his army around your walls: people who are powerful, beautiful and seemingly successful in all they undertake. When you see them, you will feel walled in like a prisoner! "And the king of Assyria sent . . . Rabshakeh . . . to king Hezekiah with a great host against Jerusalem" (2 Kings 18:17, KJV).

The first trick of the man of sin is to question a believer's commitment to trust the Lord fully. Rabshakeh was the king's ambassador; his name means "drunken envoy." He mocked the godly with his taunt: "And Rabshakeh said unto them, . . . What confidence is this wherein thou trustest? . . . Now on whom dost thou trust, that thou rebellest against me?" (2 Kings 18:19–20, KJV). The accusation was, "God is not going to get you out of this mess. You are going down! You are in real trouble, and your faith is not going to work."

Are you in a mess right now—really deep trouble? Has the devil told you that God is not going to rescue you, your faith is too weak or too little, and you're as good as dead? Perhaps you are unemployed right now, and your bills are slowly mounting. You are scared because everything looks hopeless. You hear the devil laugh, "In spite of all your love for Jesus, giving up the world, doing the right things and trusting in God, it's not going to work. You are destined to fail! You are going to end up broke, hounded by creditors and headed for suicide."

Now, listen to the devil talk in the Old Testament: "How then wilt thou turn away the face of one captain of the least of my master's servants . . .?" (Isaiah 36:9, KJV). In other words, he says, "What can you do to stop this trouble? How will you make it if you can't find a job—if you can't see even a month ahead of you, let alone your whole future? How can you possibly survive if there is an army of troubles coming in behind your present ones? Do you really believe God is going to work a miracle for you and get you out of this big mess? Give up! Here—I have a deal to offer you. . . ."

Now Satan adds a new twist: He tells you that *God* is the one behind all your troubles. Assyria's messenger claimed, "The Lord said to me, Go up against this land, and destroy it" (2 Kings 18:25, KJV). Satan will try to convince you that God is getting even with you, that He is mad at you. This is his slickest lie! He makes you believe God has forsaken you and turned you over to trouble and sorrow. He wants you to think all your problems are the result of God's punishment for your past sins. Don't believe it! It is Satan who is out to destroy you.

Our Lord is a deliverer, a fortress. Isaiah said He comes

> to appoint unto them that mourn in Zion, to give unto them beauty for ashes, the oil of joy for mourning, the garment of praise for the spirit of heaviness; that they might be called Trees of righteousness, the planting of the Lord, that he might be glorified.
>
> Isaiah 61:3

No, dear saint, you are not going down. You are simply under attack, being barraged by the enemy's lies because you have set your heart truly to trust in the Lord. Satan is trying to destroy your faith in God.

Another device Satan uses to intensify his attack on you is to try to focus your attention on his victories over other Christians. "Hath any of the gods . . . delivered . . . out of the hand of the king of Assyria? . . . Where are the gods of Hamath, and of Arpad? Have they delivered Samaria out of mine hand?" (2 Kings 18:33–34, KJV).

Satan will boast, "I am more powerful than your God. I brought down some of your biggest evangelists and seduced them into gross sin. I turned some of them into money-crazed liars. So what makes you think you can escape my power?" This same voice came to Judah from Assyria: "Who are they among all the gods of the countries, that have delivered their country out of mine hand, that the Lord should deliver Jerusalem out of mine hand?" (verse 35).

Satan will bring to your mind all the Christians who claimed to trust God but who suffered trouble, sickness and even death. He will point out some dear, old trusting saint, perhaps an elderly widow, who is always in pain and has so little to live on she seems crushed by it. The enemy will say, "She trusted God—and look what it got her! Those fallen televangelists were supposed to be close to the Lord, but look how they ended up. If preachers can't make it, how can you? What makes you think God is going to answer you when so many spiritual giants are falling?"

I know of one Pentecostal preacher who fell for this lie of the enemy. It happened one day as he sat in his minister-father's tiny mobile home. His dad was more than 75 years old, and he was ill, with no savings. He was barely scraping by financially. The younger man heard the devil whisper to him, "See how God pays his faithful shepherds? You will end up poor just like him! He led a godly life—yet he is ending it in deep poverty."

At that moment the minister told himself he would never be poor. A demonic spirit entered him, and from then on he became a wheeler-dealer, doing all he could to turn a dollar. He became involved in shady deals. He admitted he was driven by evil spirits. They haunted his every waking hour, saying, "You don't have to be poor!"

This man is still in the ministry today, but he is utterly miserable. He is losing money left and right because all his deals eventually turned sour. His dad will probably die poor yet happy in the Lord—but he himself looks likely to leave this earth full of bitterness and unbelief.

Satan Will Try to Offer You a Deal

Another of Satan's tricks is to paint a fantastic picture of what your life could be like if you make a deal with him:

> Hearken not to Hezekiah: for thus saith the king of Assyria, Make an agreement with me by a present, and come out to me, and then eat ye every man of his own vine, and every one of his fig tree, and drink ye every one the waters of his cistern: Until I come and take you away to a land like your own land, a land of corn and wine, a land of bread and vineyards, a land of oil olive and of honey, that ye may live, and not die: and hearken not unto Hezekiah, when he persuadeth you, saying, The Lord will deliver us.
>
> 2 Kings 18:31–32, KJV

The devil's voice whispers, "There's no need for you to be a nobody or to suffer unjustly. Just come out of your narrow, straight-laced ways and I'll fix things for you. You're going to prosper! I'll give you all the money you need—corn, oil, wine. No more bills, no more just making ends meet. I'll open the bank for you."

What a crooked salesman the devil is! He tells you, "Just one little deal, and all your problems will be solved. You deserve a break; you've suffered enough. Now it's your turn to make it." But don't be deceived: Every compromise you make in your walk with Jesus is the same as "going out" to the devil. When you sell short your relationship to Jesus, you are cutting a deal, making a bargain—and you are selling your soul in the process.

Satan promises, "I [will] come and take you away to a land like your own land" (verse 32). He says, in other words, "You can take God with you when you go with me. You will have to make some changes—but you will still be you. It won't hurt anything. You can have it all—Jesus *and* a deal!"

Be warned: If you buy into this lie you will be the devil's slave from that point on. There is no land of wine and oil or paradise as he promised. The minute you come out to him, he will slap chains around your neck and hands and lead you off to Babylon. You will never get what you thought you would get. Instead, you will get the whip and chain, broken promises and despair. You will get a taskmaster for a father. The satisfying water he promised you is actually poisoned. No, you won't have freedom. Instead, you will live under complete bondage, a slave to Satan's whims.

Finally, as a last resort, Satan will send you a threatening letter: "And Hezekiah received the letter of the hand of the messengers, and read it: and Hezekiah went up into the house of the Lord, and spread it before the Lord" (2 Kings 19:14, KJV).

The messenger who delivered this letter was the devil's envoy. The letter was a reproach of the living God, designed to make God's people fearful. It was the incarnation of the devil's laugh. He mocked them and said, "I am going to cut you down, make you a reproach and destroy everything in your house."

Have you received your own letter from the devil? Those divorce papers you received may have been Satan's way of saying to you, "Read it, you failure! What good does it do to serve God and deny yourself? It didn't save your marriage. It's all your fault. It could have been avoided. Phony! Failure! Give it all up!"

That pink slip on the job may also carry the devil's voice. "So that's what you get when you follow Jesus, huh? A swift kick? Nobody wants you. You're too old, too much of a has-been. You're going down, you'll lose everything. You won't have any rent money or be able to care for your family. You're finished!"

Or what about that X-ray? There it is in black and white: You have a terminal disease: AIDS! Cancer! Lupus! It's hopeless. And Satan says, "So you believe Jesus heals, do you? Well, where is He now? Why do you still have to suffer? You gave Him everything, and look what happened. He gave you nothing but continued suffering in return."

A dear friend of mine who is a businessman got a letter from the devil some time ago. It was an accountant's report showing that a trusted employee had embezzled hundreds of thousands of dollars from his company. These were the devil's words to him: "Read my lips. It does not pay to be righteous. This is what you get for giving to the Lord. You pray, you give, you walk the straight and narrow way—and you end up being embezzled. Ha! Some deal. Why don't you give it all up?"

So what do you do when you are confronted with a message from the devil? First, you have to spread the enemy's letter before the Lord, as Hezekiah did: "And Hezekiah . . . spread it before the Lord. . . . And Hezekiah prayed" (2 Kings 19:14–15, KJV).

Pray and seek the Lord. Don't ever talk or reason with the devil. Simply hold your peace, as the people in this passage did the taunting messenger: "The people held their peace, and answered him not a word: for the king's commandment was, saying, Answer him not" (2 Kings 18:36, KJV).

You see, God's response to the devil's letter is to read it and laugh! "This is the word that the Lord hath spoken concerning [the king of Assyria]; The virgin the daughter of Zion hath despised thee, and laughed thee to scorn; the daughter of Jerusalem hath shaken her head at thee" (2 Kings 19:21, KJV). In other words, God takes your letter *personally*. He said, "Devil, you didn't send that letter to My child. You sent it to *Me!*" For "whom hast thou reproached and blasphemed? and against whom hast thou exalted thy voice, and lifted up thine eyes on high? even against the Holy One of Israel" (2 Kings 19:22, KJV).

He who touches you touches the apple of God's eye. God says His loved ones are safe and that the devil cannot harm them:

> Therefore thus saith the Lord . . . He shall not come into this city, nor shoot an arrow there, nor come before it with shield, nor cast a bank against it. . . . For I will defend this city, to save it, for mine own sake, and for my servant David's sake.
>
> 2 Kings 19:32, 34, KJV

That same night God showed Hezekiah that it takes only one angel of the Lord to destroy an entire army:

And it came to pass that night, that the angel of the Lord went out, and smote in the camp of the Assyrians a hundred fourscore and five thousand: and when they arose early in the morning, behold, they were all dead corpses.

2 Kings 19:35, KJV

Remember also: "The angel of the Lord encampeth round about them that fear him, and delivereth them" (Psalm 34:7, KJV).

No matter how many demons invade, no matter how fiercely the kingdom of darkness threatens, God's people are safe. Let it sink deep into your heart of hearts: *You are safe. The Lord is set to defend and deliver you.*

The Lord Sends His Own Letter to the Devil

The Lord has written His own letter to the devil in Psalm 46. And it is so powerful that when you read it aloud, all the demons in hell will shudder and cringe in fear! It is your answer to the devil in all his attacks. It reads as follows:

Dear "man of sin":

"God is a very present help in trouble" (verse 1, KJV here and throughout). Our God is present *now*. He is our help not just in ages past but a very present help *now*, today—in the midst of any and all troubles.

"Therefore [we] will not fear" (verse 2). We have no need to fear. Our God is a consuming fire, a defender and shield for His children. Second Timothy 1:7 tells us, "God hath not given us the spirit of fear; but of power, and of love, and of a sound mind." He is altogether faithful and true to His Word.

"God is in the midst" of this temple, I cannot be moved (verse 5). My body is the temple of the Holy Spirit—and He says He is in the midst of that temple. Christ Himself makes His abode, His dwelling place, within my heart. And I *cannot* be moved or shaken! "The heathen raged, the kingdoms were moved" (verse 6). Let the heathen rage, let all the kingdoms of the earth be shaken and moved. Our God will completely destroy all demonic attackers.

"He maketh wars to cease . . . he breaketh the bow, and cutteth the spear . . . he burneth the chariot in the fire" (verse 9). He is my army against my enemies, against those who make war against me. And He Himself will completely annihilate all the devil's weapons arrayed against me: "No weapon that is formed against [the servants of the Lord] shall prosper" (Isaiah 54:17).

He says, "Be still, and know that I am God" (verse 10). I will be still and rest completely in the knowledge that *He is God.* He is my God, my Redeemer, my Defender—the sovereign Lord over all my affairs. I am safe, surrounded by His presence in the pavilion of His love. And I will stand firm and behold His majesty and glory!"

Dear saint, God provides this letter for all of Satan's attacks on your faith. Read it, meditate on it—*believe it.* It is heaven's answer to your letter from the devil.

~ 9 ~

WALKING IN THE SPIRIT

The apostle Paul commanded, "Walk in the Spirit, and ye shall not fulfil the lust of the flesh" (Galatians 5:16, KJV). He also said, "If we live in the Spirit, let us also walk in the Spirit" (verse 25). As Christians, we have heard this phrase throughout our lives: "Walk in the Spirit."

Many believers tell me they walk in the Spirit—yet they cannot tell me what that truly means. Now, let me ask you: Do *you* walk and live in the Spirit? And what does that mean to you?

I doubt that there are many of us who have even the faintest notion of what the Spirit-walk is all about. It remains a vague concept to many Christians, including ministers. But Paul makes clear how important it is to live and walk in the Spirit.

I believe "walking in the Spirit" can be defined in one sentence: It means *allowing the Holy Spirit to do in us what God sent Him to do.* And I believe that you cannot allow the Holy Spirit to do that work until you understand why God sent Him.

Jesus said of the Father,

He shall give you another Comforter, that he may abide with you for ever; even the Spirit of truth; whom the world cannot receive, because it seeth him not, neither knoweth him: but ye know him; for he dwelleth with you, and shall be in you.

John 14:16–17, KJV

The Holy Ghost has been sent down to us from the Father to accomplish one—and only one—eternal purpose. And unless we understand His mission and work in us, we will make one of two mistakes. First, we will settle for only a small portion of His work in us—such as a few of the spiritual gifts—mistakenly thinking this is His total aim and missing the grand work of His eternal purpose in our lives. Or, second, we will quench the Spirit within us and ignore Him completely, believing He is mysterious and therefore His presence is something we must take by faith and never understand.

The sad truth is the Church is often guilty of *both* of these grave mistakes! We think, "I must be walking in the Spirit, because His gifts operate in me." Yet we can operate in the gifts without walking in the Spirit. Paul says we can prophesy, heal and speak with tongues; but if we do not have love, we are nothing—we are not operating in the Spirit.

Many Christians today are convinced they are walking in the Spirit simply because they pray in tongues. They reason, "How could I pray in tongues and not be walking in the Spirit?" But praying in tongues is not necessarily praying in the Spirit. Many who wish to pray in the Spirit immediately launch out into tongues—and yet their minds are totally elsewhere! The Bible says that if you are speaking in tongues, your understanding is not fruitful. The Lord desires us both to speak with tongues *and* to pray with understanding. Praying in the Spirit can include praying in tongues—but it is so much more than that.

How many believers have been stunted in their spiritual growth because they focused on one or two particular gifts of the Spirit, yet went no further? They were somehow convinced the Holy Spirit's only work was to hand out gifts.

And how many other Christians experience the second mistake: The Holy Spirit is quenched inside them—seldom acknowledged, rarely consulted, and unable to do in them what God sent Him to do.

We acknowledge the work of Jesus Christ on the cross and we believe He abides in us and we know His presence. But we do not acknowledge the work and ministry of the Holy Spirit within us. Do you wonder what this means? It is simply this: Do you talk to the Holy Spirit as you do Jesus? Do you acknowledge Him daily?

I admit, this has been a problem for me. But I had an experience recently in which the Holy Spirit spoke to me in my prayer closet. He said, *David, acknowledge Me. Don't keep Me in some dark corner of your mind and heart. Acknowledge that I am manifesting Myself to you right now.*

A time must come when you become serious about why the Holy Spirit has been given to you. You must be able to say, "Holy Spirit, the Bible says You were sent to me as a gift from my heavenly Father. The Word says You live in me. Tell me—why have You come? What is Your eternal purpose? What are You trying to accomplish in me?"

His Eternal Purpose

The eternal purpose of the Holy Spirit in us is to bring us home to Jesus Christ as His eternal, spotless Bride.

The Holy Spirit has come to dwell in you and me to seal, sanctify, empower and prepare us—all for the bridehood of Christ. He has been sent into our world to prepare a Bride for marriage!

An Old Testament type of this relationship between believers and the Holy Spirit is found in Genesis 24. Abraham sent his eldest servant, Eliezer, to find a bride for his son Isaac. Eliezer's name means "mighty, divine helper"—a type of the Holy Spirit. And just as surely as this mighty helper came back with Rebekah to present her as a bride to Isaac, likewise the Holy Spirit will not fail to bring back a Bride for our Lord Jesus Christ.

God chose Rebekah as a bride for Isaac, and the Lord led Eliezer right to her. The servant's entire mission and purpose was focused on one thing: to bring Rebekah to Isaac—to get her to leave all she had, and to be enamored of Isaac and espoused to him. Rebekah's family recognized this. They said to Eliezer, "We see this is from the Lord. Take her and go—let her be the master's son's wife" (see Genesis 24:50–51).

And so it is with you and me. God chose us. Our salvation—our being chosen for Christ—was done by the Lord. He sent the Holy Spirit to lead us to Jesus—and if we trust Him, the Spirit will bring us safely home as Christ's eternal Bride.

Don't think for a moment you chose Christ first. You were a stranger, an alien: "Ye have not chosen me, but I have chosen you" (John 15:16, KJV). "I have chosen you out of the world, therefore the world hateth you" (verse 19). "He hath chosen us in him before the foundation of the world" (Ephesians 1:4, KJV). "God hath from the beginning chosen you to salvation through sanctification of the Spirit and belief of the truth" (2 Thessalonians 2:13, KJV).

Moses told Israel they were a special, chosen people: "For thou art a holy people unto the Lord thy God: the Lord thy God hath chosen thee to be a special people unto himself, above all people that are upon the face of the earth" (Deuteronomy 7:6, KJV). Oh, how the Israelites loved this message! They loved being chosen, being special in God's eyes.

But the problem with Israel was they wanted to enjoy the benefits of their chosenness *without taking on the obligation and discipline of becoming worthy of their Master.*

You see, Eliezer had told Rebekah, "You've been chosen. Now I will bless you with many blessings." And Rebekah put on the gold bracelets and earrings, jewels, silver and expensive clothes Eliezer had brought for her. Then Eliezer said, "Come, go with me."

Suppose Rebekah had answered, "Thank you for choosing me, and for all these blessings. But I can't go now—I'm enjoying my present place too much."

I ask you, don't we respond in much the same way today? We take all the blessings—all the gold and silver—and we accept the "chosenness." But there comes a time when we must get up and *go.*

We have to go with our Eliezer, the Holy Ghost. He tells us, "I have a divine purpose. I came with a mission from God—and I'm going to complete it!" And just as Eliezer came home with a bride for Isaac, the Holy Spirit will not come back empty-handed. The nation of Israel never got up and followed the Lord's leading to the Promised Land. They never followed the Spirit at all costs. They continued in stubborn rebellion, backslidings, spiritual harlotry and idolatry. They were chosen, but not cleansed. They were special, but they never separated themselves unto Him. And when it was time to go into Canaan, they were not ready. Instead, they were turned aside, having learned nothing in the wilderness. They were as backslidden as they had been at the beginning. What a tragedy! All that time living only for self.

This is truly a picture of modern-day Christianity. We gloat over being chosen and called of God, but we do not want the discipline of the Holy Ghost to prepare us for the holiness of the bridehood. We take all His blessings, His gold and silver and His great provision. But when the Holy Spirit says, "Let's get up and go, it's time to get prepared as a Bride for the Master"—then it's a different story.

If you were to tell me that you are saved, that you are chosen in Christ and that you love Him, I would have to ask: "Do you have a 'Rebekah heart'? Is Jesus the Lover of your soul? Is your love for Him growing and consuming your heart? Are you more hungry than ever to please Him, follow Him wherever He may lead?" Rebekah was asked, "Wilt thou go with this man? And she said, I will go" (Genesis 24:58, KJV).

His Mission

Everything the Holy Spirit does in us is related to His mission.

The Holy Spirit does not perform His work in us in some disjointed, haphazard way. He does not exist simply to help us cope with life, to get us through crises and to see us through lonely nights. He is not present in us just to pick us up and pump in a little more strength before putting us back into the race.

Everything the Holy Ghost does is related to His reason for coming, which is to bring us home as a prepared Bride. He acts only in keeping with that mission. Yes, He is our Guide, our Comforter, our Strength in time of need. But He uses every act of deliverance—every touch, every manifestation of Himself in us—to make us more suitable as a Bride.

Neither is the Holy Ghost here just to give gifts to believers. His every gift has a purpose behind it. If you prophesy, that prophecy has one purpose: to glorify Christ and to make the world and His Church fall in love with Him. Every time someone is healed, the Holy Ghost is saying, "Take a look. That's your Jesus! Isn't He wonderful? He *embodies* healing—you're seeing the manifestation of who He is!"

Indeed, those gifts are our Eliezer, saying, "Do you love Jesus? Look at what He's done for you!" Everything the Holy Spirit does points to Jesus, for the Spirit "shall not speak of himself" (John 16:13, KJV). "But when the Comforter is come, whom I will send unto you from the Father . . . *he shall testify of me*" (John 15:26, KJV).

The Holy Spirit has only one message; everything He teaches leads to one, central truth. He may shine in us like a many-splendored jewel, but every ray of truth is meant to bring us to a single truth, and it is this: "You are not your own—you have been bought with a price. You have been chosen to be espoused to Christ. And I, the Spirit of God, have been sent to reveal to you the truth that will set you free from all other loves. My truth will break every bondage to sin and deal with all unbelief. For you are not of this world; you are headed for a glorious meeting with your Espoused and are being readied for His Marriage Supper. All things are now ready—and I am preparing you! I want to present you spotless, with a passionate love in your heart for Him."

That is the work of the Holy Spirit—to manifest Jesus to the Church so that we will fall in love with Him. And, even better, that love will keep us! The Bible says if we walk in that kind of spirit, we will not fulfill the lusts of the flesh. Why? Because the Spirit is turning our hearts to Christ. He comes to open Jesus to us, to show us the beauty of His holiness.

We talk a lot about Holy-Ghost guidance. We cry out, "Lead me, Lord. Show me the way to go." Yet we do not always yield to His guidance. Instead, we spend our time trying to decide, "Did I hear the right voice? Or did I miss it? Was it just my flesh? Why didn't it work out the way I thought it should?" We become so concerned about "getting it right" that we end up not trusting the Holy Ghost at all! We do not believe He abides in us, that He has an eternal purpose, that if we will just yield to Him, *He will guide us into God's plan.*

I ask you: Why are the manifestations and gifts of the Spirit given? Paul said it was for our profit: "The manifestation of the Spirit is given to every man to profit withal" (1 Corinthians 12:7, KJV). The gift of wisdom has nothing to do with the wisdom of this world. Rather, it is wisdom in the things of Christ. Faith, healing, miracles, prophecy, discerning of spirits, tongues, interpretations— what is the profit of these gifts "withal"? It is to bring us to Christ as a Bride.

Everything the Holy Spirit does aims in that direction—and although we may forget this, the Spirit never does. Not one of these gifts has any meaning whatsoever if it is separated from the Holy Spirit's eternal purpose. Instead, it becomes only a "clanging cymbal." The operations of spiritual gifts have meaning only as they conform us to the likeness of Jesus Christ.

Have you ever been to a miracle or healing meeting? Did what you see humble you? Did it show you the "exceeding sinfulness of sin"? Did it flood your soul with love for Jesus? Did it make you long for His return? If not, then the Holy Spirit was not present because that is His work. His purpose is to draw the Bride nearer to the Bridegroom. If that did not happen, then what you saw was of the flesh. The Holy Ghost does not come to entertain, to provide signs and wonders and miracles just to thrill us or make us feel good. No, every one of His workings has this divine purpose: "I am preparing a Bride."

The work, ministry and mission of the Holy Spirit is singular: *It is to wean us from this world . . . to create a longing in us for Jesus' soon appearance . . . to convict us of everything that would blemish us . . . to turn our eyes away from everything but Jesus . . . to adorn us with the ornaments of a passionate desire to be with Him as His Bride.*

How the Holy Spirit must grieve as He beholds pastors and evangelists today turning His ministry into a circus! The Spirit cannot bear the manipulations and fleshly showmanship, all done in His name. I have heard recently about phenomenal gimmicks that have been used to try to create a sense of His presence. How grievous that must be to God's heart! Moreover, it is blasphemy against the Spirit of God.

If the Holy Spirit is at work in a church, then every song, every word of praise, every note of every instrument is given unction by the Spirit to exalt Christ. The Spirit is doing what He has been called to do—present us to our Bridegroom in all His glory and majesty. In every healing, prophecy and manifestation of God's glory in His house the Holy Spirit is at work, saying to us, "This is the love of your Espoused—this is what He is like. Isn't He wonderful? Isn't He kind, gentle, considerate, merciful? And you're seeing only a *glimpse* of Him to whom I lead you!"

Now let me show you one of the most glorious works of the Holy Spirit.

His Work

The Holy Spirit has been sent to give us a foretaste of Christ.

A foretaste is an advance taste or realization. The Bible calls it *an earnest*—"the earnest of our inheritance" (Ephesians 1:14, KJV). It means to have a taste of the whole before we have the whole. Our inheritance is Christ Himself—and the Holy Spirit brings us into His very presence as a foretaste of being received as His Bride, enjoying everlasting love and communion with Him.

Paul describes a people of God who are "sealed with that Holy

Spirit" (Ephesians 1:13, KJV). This speaks of a people specially marked by a work of the Spirit. The Holy Spirit has produced in them a distinguishing mark, a glorious inner work, something supernatural that has changed them forever. They are not ordinary believers anymore. They are no longer "of this world," since they have set their affections on things above, not on the things of this earth. They are not moved by the world's events; rather, they are unshakable. They are no longer lukewarm or halfhearted. Instead, their hearts cry out night and day, "Come quickly, Lord Jesus. . . ."

What happened to change them? What did the Holy Spirit do in these believers? What marked and sealed them forever as the Lord's possession? Simply this: *The Holy Ghost gave them a foretaste of the glory of His presence! He came to them, rolled back heaven—and they experienced a supernatural manifestation of His exceeding greatness.*

This is why it is so necessary that God's house be holy—why our hearts and hands must be clean, why we can have nothing in us to hinder the Spirit's work. It is because the Spirit of God delights in pulling back the veil, to give us a foretaste of what is coming.

Right now the Holy Spirit is opening the eyes of His chosen ones—"the eyes of your understanding being enlightened" (Ephesians 1:18, KJV). The Holy Spirit comes to a church that wants Him and is praying . . . to shepherds who are broken before God . . . to believers who have no concern other than to see the Body of Christ conformed to the image of heaven. And God is sealing such a people right now! You can go to meetings in which Jesus is so real that you taste a little bit of heaven in your soul. You come away with such a sense of *eternal reality* that your problems no longer bother you, the lapsing economy doesn't shake you, and you are especially not afraid of the devil. God puts a holy fire in your soul, and you say, "This is supernatural. This isn't me—this is God's Spirit working *in* me!"

He gives us "a little heaven" to go to heaven with—a whetting of our appetites. He opens the windows of heaven and lets us look into the glory that will be ours. We get a taste of His holiness, His peace, His rest, His love—and we are forever spoiled for this earth, because we yearn for the fullness of what we have tasted.

His Completed Mission

The Spirit's mission is not complete until He creates in us a passionate, ever-increasing yearning for Christ.

What kind of Bride do you think the Spirit will present to Jesus Christ on that day of Revelation? One who is halfhearted? Whose love is lukewarm, or cold? Who is not devoted to Jesus? Who does not want intimacy with Christ?

If you truly love Jesus, He is never out of your mind. He is present in your every waking moment. Some Christians think, "That will happen after I die. When I get to heaven, everything will change. I'll become the special Bride of the Lord then." No—dying doesn't sanctify anybody! The Holy Ghost is here today, He is alive and working in you—to produce in you a passionate love for Christ on *this* side of death.

Romans 8:26 describes one of the most powerful works of the Holy Spirit in the heart of the believer: "Likewise the Spirit also helpeth our infirmities: for we know not what we should pray for as we ought: but the Spirit itself maketh intercession for us with groanings which cannot be uttered." What is this groaning of the Holy Spirit deep inside the heart? What is this emotion that is so profound there are no words to express it?

The Hebrew word used for *groaning* means "a yearning"—a longing for more of Christ. You can yearn after Jesus so much that you sit in His presence and nothing comes out but a deep groaning, something that cannot be uttered. It says, "Jesus, You're the only happiness there is in this world. I have tasted and seen that You are good—and I want *all* of You."

This is the deep, inner cry of someone who hungers for holiness and is anguished over his iniquities. Yet he admits, "I don't know how to pray. I don't know what to pray for, or as I should." His heart's cry is: "Holy Spirit, come! You know the mind of God. You know how to pray according to the will of the Father. Walk with me—take control!"

The mark of one who walks in the Spirit is that he has an insatiable appetite for Jesus. It is not just because he is sick of all the garbage he sees in the world—all the filth, crime, drugs and unemployment. No, rather, it is something very positive. Like Paul, he is simply anxious to depart and be with the Lord. He is being moved upon by the Spirit to pursue Christ with such passion and emotion that He is overwhelmed. His heart so longs for Christ that no words can express his hunger and love. It is a marvelous, powerful experience—yet it is also painful, because he cannot yet come into the fullness that awaits him!

Sadly, few today have this longing for Christ. There is little hungering or thirsting, and so little passion. Each Sunday churches are packed with Christians *who never question or examine their love for Christ.*

But the Holy Ghost has found His people. They are allowing the Spirit to take control. They are beginning to yield to Him—and the more they do, the more His inner groaning comes forth. I ask you: What has happened in your life since you got saved? Are you just going through the motions? Are you lukewarm? Are you afraid to be set "on fire" for the Lord because you will be considered a fanatic?

Ask the Holy Ghost so to reveal Christ to your heart that you will be totally weaned from this world. That's what happened to Abraham. He said, "I'm only passing through here." He was looking for a city whose builder and maker was God. He had a vision, and his eyes were opened to eternity.

Can you say right now that you are ready to go be with Him, that you want Him more than your very life? You may say that often—but do you mean it when you sing, "He's more than life to me"? Are you more passionately in love with Jesus than when you first met Him?

Right now, the Holy Spirit may be poking at the dying embers of your love. It is because He desires to set your heart aflame for the Bridegroom. Are you allowing the Spirit of God to convict you of sin and unbelief? If so, rejoice! He wants you to be cleansed from every spot or wrinkle on that day when you meet your Bridegroom. Yield to His leading. Let Him do His work in you completely—and you will truly know what it means to walk in the Spirit.

~ 10 ~
MANIFESTING THE PRESENCE
OF JESUS

If you were to ask any Christian, "Do you love Jesus?" the answer you would most likely hear is, "Yes, absolutely!" What believer would answer of himself otherwise?

But words alone will not stand in the holy light of God's Word. Jesus said two distinct things reveal your love for Him. And if these two things are not evident in your life, then your love for Jesus is in word alone and not in deed and truth. These two evidences are: 1) Your obedience to Jesus' every command, and 2) manifesting His presence in your life.

This verse says it all: "He that hath my commandments, and keepeth them, he it is that loveth me . . . and I will love him, and will manifest myself to him" (John 14:21, KJV). We know what it means to keep Christ's commandments. But what does it mean that He will "manifest" Himself to us?

Manifest means to "shine or break forth." It means, in other words, that we are to become an instrument or channel that radiates Christ's presence. The Church often prays, "O Lord, send us Your presence. Come among us, fall upon us, move upon us, reveal

Yourself to us!" But God's presence does not just "come down." It does not suddenly fall and surprise or overwhelm the congregation. We seem to have the idea that Christ's presence is an invisible smoke that God sprays into the atmosphere, like the Old Testament glory-cloud that so filled the Temple that the priests could not stand to minister.

We forget too easily that, in this day, our bodies are the temple of the Lord: "Know ye not that your body is the temple of the Holy Ghost which is in you?" (1 Corinthians 6:19, KJV). And if His glory comes, it must appear in our hearts and fill our bodies. Christ does not inhabit buildings or a certain atmosphere; in fact, the very heavens cannot contain Him. Rather He is manifested through our obedient, sanctified bodies, which are His temples: "For ye are the temple of the living God; as God hath said, I will dwell in them, and walk in them; and I will be their God, and they shall be my people" (2 Corinthians 6:16, KJV).

But why is there little or no presence of Jesus in the midst of our churches? Why are so many congregations dead? Because either the pastor or the people—or both—are spiritually dead! Experiencing the presence of Jesus in a church is not so much a corporate matter as it is an individual one. True, a spiritually lifeless, prayerless shepherd can spread death over the congregation. Yet every member is still a temple and remains personally responsible to obey God and to be available as an instrument of His presence. Your church can be dead, and yet you still can be full of Christ's presence.

A few short years ago, four teenage boys told me, "You preached in our church last year, and it was dead. So we four started a prayer meeting just for us. We wanted to get right with God, to repent and be on fire for Jesus. Our group grew to ten, and we helped other fellows get saved. Now we're inviting the deacons and pastors to come and pray with us. We really have a changed church. The Lord is there now!"

A true revival, as I see it, is a restoration of this kind of intense love for Jesus. This love is marked by a new desire to obey His every word, a heart attitude that says, "whatever He says, I will do." Indeed, a revival is a return to obedient love by a people who have individually confessed and forsaken all sin, desiring only to become channels of Christ's presence. True revival is embodied in such people. They carry Christ's glory and presence with them, because His life flows through them at all times.

Pastors of large churches have said to me, "You must come and see what God is doing. Thousands are coming—we're packed out. Our worship is really something to behold!" I have gone to some of these churches with great expectations, but seldom have I sensed or experienced the actual presence of Jesus in their mass meetings. The congregations exhibited no true repentance. I believe that if a prophet had stood up and exposed the divorce, adultery, fornication and mixture with evil music that existed in those churches, half the crowd would have walked out.

I left these meetings knowing in my heart that Jesus was not among the people. It was clear they did not live in obedience to Him, so in truth they could not be loving Him. Jesus will *not* manifest Himself to those who say they have love but do not obey. Wherever you find the presence of Jesus, you always will find at least five manifestations breaking forth among His people:

1. God's people manifest a deep, smiting conviction of sin.

Wherever holy vessels embody the living presence of Jesus, and His holy presence bursts forth from obedient hearts, the person who harbors sin in his life will do one of two things: either fall down and confess, or run and hide! A day is coming when Jesus will reveal Himself fully to wicked mankind. And when that takes place, as the book of Revelation foretells, people will try desperately to hide from His awesome presence: "[They] hid themselves in the dens and in the rocks of the mountains; and said to the mountains and rocks, Fall on us, and hide us from the face of him that sitteth on the throne" (Revelation 6:15–16, KJV).

During one Tuesday night service at Times Square Church, I was overwhelmed as the presence of Jesus became real through the godly worshipers waiting upon Him. People came to the altar, some weeping. The fear of the Lord was awesome. I felt like Isaiah who said, "Woe is me! for I am . . . a man of unclean lips, and I dwell

109

in the midst of a people of unclean lips" (Isaiah 6:5, KJV). At our church we often preach against sin, and many can say, "I've laid down everything the Spirit has exposed in me that's unlike Jesus." But sitting under convicting sermons alone will not bring the hatred for sin that so many need in these last days. It is going to take deep, piercing manifestations of God's holy presence. It is while in His holy presence that we learn to hate sin and to walk in His fear.

I hear Christians boast, "On that Day of Judgment, I will not have to fall on my face. I will stand boldly, warts and all, because I am trusting in His salvation, not in my works!" It is true that we are not saved by works. But if we do not obey Christ's commandments, then we never really loved Him, and He was not manifested in us (see John 14:21).

The apostle John, our "brother, and companion in tribulation" (Revelation 1:9), the one who once leaned on Jesus' breast, saw Christ in His glorified holiness. John testified,

> I turned . . . [and] I saw . . . one like unto the Son of man. . . . His eyes were as a flame of fire . . . his voice as the sound of many waters. . . . And his countenance was as the sun shineth in his strength. And when I saw him, I fell at his feet as dead. And he laid his right hand upon me, saying unto me, Fear not.
>
> Revelation 1:12–17, KJV

You may be as John was, a righteous brother or sister in the Lord, a servant who has endured much tribulation. But can any of us stand before a Presence that shines as the sun in all its strength? We will no more be able to look upon that holiness than we can now look into the sun without tinted glasses. He will have to enable us in that day, to touch us and reassure us not to be afraid. He "is able to keep you from falling, and to present you faultless before the presence of his glory with exceeding joy" (Jude 24, KJV).

2. God's people manifest the power to destroy sin.

Let God arise, let his enemies be scattered: let them also that hate him flee before him. As smoke is driven away, so drive them away: as wax melteth before the fire, so let the wicked perish at the presence of God.

Psalm 68:1–2, KJV

This passage is a picture of what ought to happen when you get alone with God in your prayer closet. His awesome, manifest presence is like a hurricane that blows away the dirt and smoke of lust. Like a blazing fire, it melts down all hardness. Wickedness perishes in His presence.

"The hills melted like wax at the presence of the Lord" (Psalm 97:5, KJV). The hills in this psalm represent satanic strongholds and mountains of stubbornness, all of which melt away from those who are shut in with God. We can pray until we are exhausted, "O God, send Your sin-exposing, sin-destroying power to all our churches!" But it will not do any good until the Spirit raises up in those churches a praying, holy remnant whose pure hearts invite His presence into the sanctuary. You will not experience the real presence of Jesus until you have within you a growing hatred for sin, a piercing conviction for your failures and a deepening sense of the exceeding sinfulness of sin. Those without Christ's presence become less and less convicted by sin. And the further they withdraw from His presence, the bolder, more arrogant and more comfortable in compromise they grow.

Yet it is not enough for us to eat and drink in His presence. We must also be changed and purified by being with Him.

Then shall ye begin to say, We have eaten and drunk in thy presence, and thou hast taught in our streets. But he shall say, I tell you, I know you not whence ye are; depart from me, all ye workers of iniquity.

Luke 13:26–27, KJV

Those who confess that they have eaten and drunk in His presence will really be saying, "We were in Your presence, we sat under Your teaching." Thus they will be judged out of their own mouths. They will admit that they sat in His presence—but they were not changed. They remained blind to their own sinfulness, hardened and unaffected by the presence of Christ. Jesus will answer them, "I don't know you—depart from Me!"

How dangerous it is to sit among saints of God who radiate His glory and presence, to whom Jesus reveals Himself so powerfully, and not be changed! How deadly not to see the ugliness of sin, the plague of the heart! Will you dare tell the Lord, "I attended a church where Your presence was real—I sat in Your holy presence"? This will seal your own destruction. It would be better for you never to have known His presence.

3. God's people manifest a spirit of holiness.

"[Jesus was] declared to be the Son of God with power, according to the spirit of holiness" (Romans 1:4, KJV).

True holiness has a spirit operating behind it. Wherever you find the presence of Jesus working in or among His people, you will discover much more in them than obedience, separation from the world and abstinence from ungodly things. You will find a *spirit* of obedience.

To these people, obedience is no longer just a matter of doing what is right and avoiding what is wrong. The believer who delights in pleasing the Lord has a spirit resting upon him that automatically draws him to the light.

> For every one that doeth evil hateth the light, neither cometh to the light, lest his deeds should be reproved. But he that doeth truth cometh to the light, that his deeds may be made manifest, that they are wrought in God.
>
> John 3:20–21, KJV

Those who harbor hidden sin possess a spirit of deviousness. This is a secretive spirit that hates reproof and seeks to cover hidden corruption.

A holy person is not afraid of the light of God's presence. Rather, he *invites* that glaring light, because a spirit of holiness within him cries out, "I want all hidden things to be brought out! I want to be as much like Jesus as is possible for a human being on this earth." This servant runs to the light, and when he surrenders, the light of Christ's presence becomes pure glory to him.

When the presence of Jesus is manifested, it exposes all secrets and brings all hidden things into the open. God's people forsake all darkness and become open books, to be "read of all men" (2 Corinthians 3:2, KJV). Listen to the language of the spirit of holiness: "We keep his commandments, and do those things that are pleasing in his sight" (1 John 3:22, KJV). In the Greek translation, these words are very strong: "We keep His commandments, holding to them with *great excitement*, because we know it pleases Him!"

Here is how I believe this spirit of holiness operates in a church where the presence of Jesus is manifested:

First of all, brothers and sisters come to your church in victory with the smiles of overcomers. They testify, "I'm being changed! The Lord is putting a desire in my heart to obey Him and walk blameless before His presence." And as you witness this, your spirit rejoices, saying within, "Thank God, these servants are bringing Him pleasure! My brothers and my sisters are making heaven rejoice!" Your excitement extends *beyond* the freedom we presently enjoy, and *beyond* our rescue from the devil's power. It stems from the fact that, more than all else, *you are becoming a body that is learning how to please Him.* You obey not out of duty nor out of fear, but because a spirit of obedience lives inside you. You delight in Christ's joy, rejoicing that His heart rejoices! This is true holiness.

4. God's people manifest a sharing of the Lord's burden.

Every true burden that the Lord has given me to bear has been borne out of a deep, life-changing encounter in the presence of Jesus. Nearly 35 years ago the Spirit of God came on me in a spirit of weeping. I sold my television, which dominated my free time, and

113

for a year I shut myself in with the Lord in prayer. I spent months praying in my study and in the woods, and while I was in His presence, He opened His heart to me and showed me a whole suffering world. Out of this came the command, *Go to New York.* I obeyed, and while I walked these streets He shared with me His burden for gangs, addicts and alcoholics.

Several years ago, God called me to a life of much deeper communion. I spent months alone with Jesus, being purged, laying down all ambition, wanting only to please Him. Then came this command: *Go back to New York.* Now our ministry moves only through prayer and by being in His presence. The burden we have must be *His* burden, or it is all in vain.

When I was a child, camp meetings were popular. At that time there were no Christian campgrounds or retreats; tents and little cabins were all that churches could afford. In later years Gwen and I used to go to one called "Living Waters Camp" in Cherry Tree, Pennsylvania. People would come to that camp full of God's presence. We had no TVs, and no one dared even to think about going to the theater. Jesus was our everything!

The meetings would last until late in the night. It was in just such a meeting when I was eight years old that Jesus shone forth so mightily we all ran to the altar. I remember kneeling in the straw, and while I was in God's presence He became my life. He spoke to me there, saying, *Give Me your life!* I lay for hours, weeping and trembling at that camp-meeting altar. And when I stood up God's hand was on my life and His burden was on my soul. I doubt if I would be ministering today if not for the dear saints who came to those camp meetings so full of Jesus. They manifested His glory.

No one shared the burden of the Lord more than the apostle Paul. Jesus laid on his shoulders the yoke of His own heart. But how did Paul receive that burden? From an encounter with the bright sun of Christ's presence: "Suddenly there shined round about him a light from heaven: and he fell to the earth" (Acts 9:3–4, KJV). This was the very presence of Jesus, and Paul's ministry came out of that encounter. Notice that the command, "Arise, and go" (verse 6), came next. When you have the actual, living presence of Jesus, you don't need committees, strategies or how-to seminars for direction. The Holy Ghost comes and says, "Go here . . . go there . . . do it this way. . . ." He tells you when, where and how.

You may hear two ministers, each sincere, each preaching the same message. The doctrine of both may be right, and each one may preach with gusto. Yet the words of one are lifeless and fall on deaf ears; nothing results. But the words of the other prick the heart like a sword. This preacher shares and reveals the true burden of the Lord because he has been shut in with Jesus and can speak what is on his Lord's heart. God's presence through him brings both conviction and life.

Show me a minister who is shut in with Christ, waiting in His presence, and I will show you one who never misses the mind of Christ. If he takes one step out of line, the Lord brings him back. Likewise, show me a church that obeys God's Word and manifests His presence, and I'll show you a church body that hears from God, knows His burden and does only what pleases Him. Such a body lets the striving crowd pass by. They will hear a thousand voices of good causes and promotions saying, "Come, help us!" Yet they will not move until *He* says move. This church will pursue no cause if His presence is not in it.

5. God's people manifest an exuberant and exceedingly great joy.

"Thou hast made known to me the ways of life; thou shalt make me full of joy with thy countenance" (Acts 2:28, KJV). Have you ever wondered what Jesus was like from day to day—what His heart and His attitude were? Did He look crushed by all the burdens He carried? Did He weep a great deal? Was there a solemn heaviness in His presence?

He did weep, and He did carry heavy burdens. In Gethsemane He sweat drops of blood, and at other times He groaned and sighed over unbelief. But the Word of God makes it clear Christ was full of joy and gladness:

For David speaketh concerning him, I foresaw the Lord always before my face; for he is on my right hand, that I should not be moved [troubled]: Therefore did my heart rejoice, and my tongue was glad. . . . Thou hast made known to me the ways of life; thou shalt make me full of joy with thy countenance.

Acts 2:25–28, KJV

In speaking this to the council of the Jews, Stephen quoted a prophecy from Psalm 16. It was a vision of Christ who had a rejoicing heart, a tongue speaking gladness and a countenance full of joy because of the presence of His Father. Likewise, we are to rejoice, be glad and full of joy for the same reasons—specifically four of them—that Jesus is joyful.

The first reason is that He knew it was impossible for death to hold Him. *And so it is for us!* This knowledge destroys the wicked doctrine that says Jesus was placed in the devil's hands and had to fight His way out of hell. Jesus knew on earth that death could not hold Him—and so do we.

Second, the Lord is at our right hand in all our troubles. We can rest hopefully and expectantly, knowing He is beside us at all times.

Third, "Thou will not leave my soul in hell [death]!" We will rise to new life in a new body, in a new world.

And fourth, *His very presence floods us with joy!* How can we do anything but shout and be glad when we have been delivered from hell, promised eternal life, given His assurance in all troubles here on earth and have His presence manifested before us?

At times we must be still and know He is God. Sometimes the Spirit brings forth sweet, melodic love songs to Jesus. But throughout God's Word, whenever He brought victory over enemies, the people always lifted up a great shout, a loud noise of praise to the Lord. On the seventh day that Israel marched around Jericho, this commandment circulated: "All the people shall shout with a great shout; and the wall of the city shall fall down flat" (Joshua 6:5, KJV). "And the people shouted with a great shout, that the wall fell down flat" (verse 20, KJV).

In Ezra we discover that another great shout took place when the Temple foundation was laid.

> When the builders laid the foundation of the temple of the Lord, . . . they sang together . . . in praising and giving thanks unto the Lord. . . . And all the people shouted with a great shout, when they praised the Lord . . . so that the people could not discern the noise of the shout of joy from the noise of the weeping of the people: for the people shouted with a loud shout, and the noise was heard afar off.
>
> Ezra 3:10–11, 13, KJV

The Hebrew word used for *shout* here means "split the ears." The weeping of the Israelites was so joyful, and the praises so loud, that it was ear-splitting!

God wants us to know His word on this matter. *Noise* in Hebrew, suggests "thunder, sparks, fire." The Psalms command us: "Make a joyful noise unto God, all ye lands" (Psalm 66:1, KJV). "Sing aloud unto God our strength: make a joyful noise unto the God of Jacob" (Psalm 81:1, KJV).

> Make a joyful noise unto the Lord, all the earth: make a loud noise, and rejoice, and sing praise. . . . With trumpets and sound of cornet make a joyful noise before the Lord, the King. . . . Let the floods clap their hands: let the hills be joyful together.
>
> Psalm 98:4, 6, 8, KJV

God's people know exceeding great joy whenever the presence of Jesus has been revealed. And if we will not shout His praises, the trees will do it for us. In the words of a praise song, we can "sing till the power of the Lord comes down!"

If you hunger for Jesus alone, you *will* experience the manifestation of His presence.

SECTION 2

THE COST OF HUNGERING

~ 11 ~
THE COST OF GOING ALL THE WAY WITH GOD

One of the fastest ways to lose friends is to go all the way with God. Once you become serious about spiritual matters—forsaking all your idols, taking your eyes off the things of this world, turning to Jesus with all of your heart and hungering for more of Him—you suddenly become "a religious fanatic." And soon you'll experience the worst rejection of your lifetime.

Why this change?

When you were a lukewarm Christian you were no trouble to anyone, not even the devil. You were neither overly sinful nor overly holy. You were just another of many halfhearted believers, and your life was quiet and untroubled. You were accepted. But then you changed. You got hungry for more of Jesus and you could no longer play church games. You repented and turned to the Lord with all your heart. Down came your idols of money, fame, pleasure, sports—anything and everything that was more important to you than Jesus. You began to dig into God's Word. You stopped pursuing material possessions and became obsessed with pursuing Christ. You entered a new realm of discernment and began to see things in the Church that before had never bothered you. You heard things from the pulpit that broke your heart. You saw other Christians compromising as you once did, and it hurt you. In short, you were awakened, turned around, made broken and contrite in spirit, and God gave you a burden for His Church.

And the result? Now your friends and family think you're crazy. Instead of rejoicing with you or encouraging you, they ridicule you, mock you and call you a fanatic. "What's happened to you?" they say. "We don't even know who you are anymore. Why don't you go back to the way you used to be?"

If you've experienced this, don't be discouraged—you're in good company. Let's look at several Old and New Testament faithful who knew just what you're feeling.

Moses, for instance, was touched wonderfully by God, and was awakened in his heart concerning the bondage of His people. In fact, Moses was so excited by this great revelation of deliverance that he ran to share it: "It came into his heart to visit his brethren. . . . For he supposed his brethren would have understood how that God by his hand would deliver them: but they understood not" (Acts 7:23, 25, KJV).

Moses and his vision were spurned. But why? Moses was the meekest man on earth, consumed with God. He was not acting holier-than-thou; he was acting prophetically according to God's will. He only wanted his brothers and sisters to hear and see what God was about to do. But his spirituality offended them. They rejected him, saying, "Who made you a ruler and judge over us? Who do you think you are?"

A few years ago the Holy Spirit awakened me and I began to embrace the Lord's call to holiness. I got serious about walking in God's truth, and His Word became life to me. I began to see things I'd never seen before, and I wanted to share them with everybody. I called ministers on the phone and explained what God was saying to me. Many came to my office to see me. I opened up my Bible to them, weeping, and pointed out the glorious truths of full surrender and heart purity.

I thought these ministers of God would see these truths, too

—that they would love the Word and fall on their knees with me to pray for a new touch of God. Instead, most of them just blinked and looked puzzled. They said things like, "Are you sure you aren't going a little overboard?" or, "That's a little heavy for me." The more I sought God, the less I saw of them. It was as if they were throwing cold water in my face. They didn't want to hear anything the Lord had shared with me.

What to Expect

Again, if this has happened to you since God awakened you, you are not alone. God's Word warns you what to expect if you are determined to go all the way with Him. You can expect any or all of three reactions: 1. You will be rejected. 2. You will be cast out. 3. You will be stoned.

1. You will be rejected.

Jesus warned, "If you were of the world, the world would love its own. Yet because you are not of the world, but I chose you out of the world, therefore the world hates you" (John 15:19). Show me a believer who has become both a lover and a doer of the truth, and I'll show you one who has been rejected and persecuted by the entire lukewarm Church. Rest assured, if you give up on this world, it will quickly give up on you.

Jesus had many followers—that is, until the word He preached was perceived to be too hard and demanding. The miracle-loving crowd heard His claims and forsook Him, saying, "This is too hard! Who can receive it?" Then Jesus turned to His disciples and asked, "Will you also turn away?" or, in other words, "Is My word too hard for you, too?" Peter answered, "Lord, to whom shall we go? You have the words of eternal life" (John 6:68). No, Peter and the rest of the disciples would not walk away. They loved the word that most people said was too harsh and demanding; they knew it was producing in them eternal values. They wanted to follow the truth, no matter what the cost.

This is the question every Christian must face in these last days:

Will we turn aside from truth that convicts us—that points out our sins and commands us to tear down our idols? Will we ignore truth that tells us to take our eyes off materialism, off the things of this world and off ourselves? Will we allow the Holy Spirit to probe and expose us?

Every lover and doer of truth desires to come to the light, to have every secret deed exposed. Jesus said, "For everyone practicing evil hates the light and does not come to the light, lest his deeds should be exposed. But he who does the truth comes to the light, that his deeds may be clearly seen, that they have been done in God" (John 3:20–21).

Genuine truth always exposes every hidden thing. When Jesus began to shed His light on the hidden sins of the religious Jews, they sought to kill Him. Jesus said, "I know that you are Abraham's descendants, but you seek to kill Me, because My word has no place in you" (John 8:37). "You seek to kill Me, a Man who has told you the truth" (verse 40). "He who is of God hears God's words; therefore you do not hear, because you are not of God" (verse 47).

Multitudes of Christians today do not love the truth. God says it is because they hide their sin and secretly take pleasure in unrighteousness. These compromising pleasure-lovers are deceived but, like the Jews of Jesus' day, they are convinced they see clearly. They believe that they are God's children, but they reject ferociously every word that exposes their deep, inner secrets and lusts. Something other than truth holds their hearts; they do not embrace God's Word like a priceless pearl. Instead they coddle whatever that thing is—a hidden pleasure, idol, sin or false teaching that caters to their flesh.

But a day of reckoning is coming. The Bible says that those who turn a deaf ear to the truth will soon miss it altogether:

And then the lawless one will be revealed, whom the Lord will consume with the breath of His mouth and destroy with the brightness of His coming. The coming of the lawless one is according to the working of Satan, with all power, signs, and lying wonders, and with all unrighteous deception among those who perish, because they did not receive the love of the truth, that they might be saved. And for this reason God will send them strong delusion, that they should believe the lie, that they all may be condemned who did not believe the truth but had pleasure in unrighteousness.

2 Thessalonians 2:8–12

You must understand that those who reject you and forsake you because of truth have good reason: It is because they see you as a threat to something they hold dear. Your separated life is a rebuke to their compromise and lukewarmness.

Paul experienced this numerous times. He wrote to Timothy, "All those in Asia have turned away from me" (2 Timothy 1:15). The apostle had given his all to these people, declaring to them the whole counsel of God. He was blameless before them, holy and unrebukable. Yet the churches of Asia rejected him and his own spiritual children avoided him. Why? Because Paul was now in prison. He was suffering—in deep affliction, bound by chains, "a prisoner of the Lord." In the meantime, a new teacher had become popular, one who brought an ear-tickling message to the people Paul had taught. "Alexander the coppersmith did me much harm," the apostle wrote. "May the Lord repay him according to his works" (2 Timothy 4:14).

Alexander and Hymenaeus were teaching a false gospel that catered to the flesh. Their doctrines denied all suffering and hardship. Alexander's name means "man-pleaser." Hymenaeus was named after the god of weddings; he represented a gospel of love, blessings, joy, celebration and man-pleasing without holiness. Scripture says Paul turned these men over to Satan that they might learn to stop blaspheming (1 Timothy 1:20). This was for the destruction not of their bodies, but of their flesh-doctrines.

Paul said these two men shipwrecked true faith by excusing sin, for they themselves did not have pure consciences, and the result was man-pleasing doctrine. Alexander and Hymenaeus had rejected Paul because he was in prison, which they perceived to be a spiritual loss of freedom. They viewed his chains as a lack of faith; they believed the devil held Paul prisoner. They thought, *If Paul is so holy, and if he preaches God as so all-powerful, then why is he suffering?* To those who believed Christians don't have to suffer, Paul's prison stay was embarrassing.

Today we still have such people-pleasers among us. Many Christians will reject you and be ashamed of you as you endure trials, tribulations and sickness. They'll think it's all happening because you don't have enough faith, or because you haven't received the "revelation" that they have about sickness and suffering.

2. You will be cast out.

Jesus warned His disciples of the further rejection they would face: "They will put you out of the synagogues; yes, the time is coming that whoever kills you will think that he offers God service" (John 16:2). Jesus was saying, "I'm telling you these things so you won't stumble. Don't be surprised when the lukewarm church throws you out, because they don't know the Father or Me."

Christ once healed a young man who was born blind. When this man's eyes were opened, he became overjoyed—he could see! The religious Pharisees brought this man in to interrogate him. Yet all he told them was, "One thing I know: that though I was blind, now I see" (John 9:25). And in response to their probing about Jesus, he added a further revelation: "If this Man were not from God, He could do nothing" (John 9:33). Did the religious leaders rejoice over this man's newfound vision? No! They thought it absurd that one who was "completely born in sins" would be teaching them by his testimony, and they cast him out of the synagogue (John 9:34).

This young man who was healed of blindness represents the holy remnant whose eyes are now being opened to the holiness of God. Go ahead and testify as he did, giving glory to God: "Once I was blind, and now I see!" But be forewarned: Those who don't want to hear of your new vision will cast you out also, saying, "Who made you our teacher?"

If you intend to go all the way with Christ, you must be prepared to bear His sufferings: "If the world hates you, you know that it hated Me before it hated you. . . . All these things they will do to you for My name's sake, because they do not know Him who sent

Me" (John 15:18, 21). Who reproached Jesus, heaped shame upon His head and vilified His name as filthy? It was the man-centered religious crowd! Just as Christ walked in this world and was subject to its rejection, so are you. If the world persecuted and reproached Him, they will do the same to all who die to self for His sake.

This is one reaction from the "religious crowd." But you may also find that just the opposite is true from another segment of church life: If you are in a church that is lukewarm, the people likely won't criticize what *anyone* thinks.

I have heard hungry Christians say, "My church is dead. What shall I do?" Their answer can be found in the book of Acts. The apostle Paul went into every new synagogue he encountered and tried hard to persuade any lukewarm churchgoers about Christ, hoping they would hear. But the people's response was to expel Paul from the region.

Hear this warning: Do as Paul did and get out! He "shook off the dust from [his] feet against them" (Acts 13:51). Paul said to these religious Jews, "It was necessary that the word of God should be spoken to you first; but since you reject it . . . we turn to the Gentiles" (Acts 13:46).

If you are in a fellowship or church that has heard the truth and has turned aside, "Lo, leave it." You are not going to change anything—but they may change you! "What communion has light with darkness?. . . 'Come out from among them and be separate, says the Lord. Do not touch what is unclean, and I will receive you' " (2 Corinthians 6:14, 17).

3. You will be stoned.

If you hold fast to your commitment to Jesus, even in the face of being rejected and cast out, the same man-centered majority will stand ready to stone you: "And they stoned Stephen as he was calling on God and saying, Lord Jesus, receive my spirit" (Acts 7:59). Who stoned Stephen? The most prestigious religious council of the day (see Acts 6:12). Stephen stood against the entire religious system!

Here was Stephen, a man who had his eyes fixed on Jesus yet who was hated by men who supposedly loved God. Listen to the venom of these religious leaders: "When they heard these things they were cut [furious] to the heart, and they gnashed at him with their teeth" (Acts 7:54). "They . . . stopped their ears, and ran at him with one accord" (verse 57). What was it about this righteous man that so angered the religious multitudes? It was that he preached truth that cut them to the heart: "You stiff-necked and uncircumcised in heart and ears! You always resist the Holy Spirit; as your fathers did, so do you" (verse 51). "[You] have received the law . . . and have not kept it" (verse 53).

These leaders' hearts still clung to the world, bound as they were by lust. They knew God's Law but they refused to obey it. Now the two-edged sword of truth had cut to the deepest part of their hearts. Stephen's testimony of an open heaven finally brought down their wrath upon him:

> But he, being full of the Holy Spirit, gazed into heaven and saw the glory of God, and Jesus standing at the right hand of God, and said, "Look! I see the heavens opened and the Son of Man standing at the right hand of God!" Then they cried out with a loud voice, stopped their ears, and ran at him with one accord; and they cast him out of the city and stoned him.
>
> Acts 7:55–58

This stoning will not likely take a literal form in your life. Think of it this way: Today, in this age of grace, if a man looks upon a woman with lust, in God's eyes he is committing adultery. If someone hates, he is a murderer. Conversely, if vicious words are hurled at you for going all the way with God, you are being stoned: "[They] sharpen their tongue like a sword, and bend their bows to shoot their arrows—bitter words" (Psalm 64:3).

Jesus taught a parable of a householder who owned a vineyard. At harvest time this vineyard owner sent his servants for the fruit, but the one in charge of the vineyard took the servants, beat one, killed another and stoned another (see Matthew 21:35). And so it happens today as well. God has sent out his Holy watchmen to gather in the fruit of His vineyard. But instead of being heard and accepted, these watchmen have met with verbal abuse, hatred and stoning with sharp words.

It was no different for Joshua and Caleb in the story of the spies told in Numbers 13–14. The Israelites wanted to stone them for calling upon the people to go all the way with God into the land of Canaan. Joshua and Caleb declared boldly, "Let us go up at once and take possession of the land, for we are well able to overcome it!" but the other spies would hear none of it. They said, "There are too many giants, too many high walls. Let us choose a leader and return to Egypt."

As Moses fell on his face in grief at this expression of unbelief, Joshua and Caleb warned the people not to rebel against the Lord or fear the people of the land. They spoke assuredly that the Lord would be with them. Yet here was the response of the people: "All the congregation said to stone them with stones. Now the glory of the Lord appeared in the tabernacle of meeting before all the children of Israel. Then the Lord said to Moses: 'How long will these people reject Me?' " (Numbers 14:10–11).

Why would a call to obedience provoke such a reaction in them? Because compromise and unbelief go hand in hand. Once the heart is captured by an idol or lust, unbelief takes hold. And after that happens, all preaching against compromise grates on one's conscience; that person ends up fighting God, even while blindly confessing His name.

I believe that, like Stephen, we can say, "I see heaven open!" Like Joshua and Caleb and Moses we can warn, "Don't rebel against the Lord!" We can have a clear vision of Jesus—a cutting word of truth—and we can be sure it will evoke the wrath of those uncircumcised of heart.

What Is Our Response?

How shall we react when rejected, cast out and stoned? We shall follow the example of our Master, Jesus, the Lamb who "opened not His mouth." His actions say this to us: Do not call down fire out of heaven upon those who heap abuse on you. "Pray for those who spitefully use you" (Matthew 5:44). "Being reviled, we bless; being persecuted, we endure" (1 Corinthians 4:12).

I have no sympathy for arrogant, self-styled prophets who fight back, threaten or throw curses about. In the Old Testament, Shimei stood on a hill throwing stones at David as the king retreated from Jerusalem and from his rebellious son Absalom. David's army captain said, "Why should this dead dog curse my lord the king? Please, let me go over and take off his head!" But David answered, "Let him alone, and let him curse. . . . It may be that the Lord will look on my affliction, and that the Lord will repay me with good for his cursing this day" (2 Samuel 16:9–12).

Scripture says that when Moses went all the way up to the mountain and shut himself up with God, his face shone. Although the others saw it, Moses did not know it. Eventually he put a veil over his face, but he had not even been aware of the reflection of God's holiness upon him. And, like Stephen, Moses did not flaunt his touch from God. These men did not put on airs, professing to be prophets; they did not threaten. They did not speak of having "new" or "special" revelation. They did not put on a display of false piety. Humility is the mark of the soul who is totally dependent on Christ. That person has no spiritual pride, no hint of an attitude of exclusiveness.

You see, we face a cost for going all the way with Jesus, but we also will receive a reward: *It is simply the blessing of having Christ stand with us.* There are many other rewards as well (see Matthew 19:29), but I mention this one because it is all we will ever need.

When Paul was imprisoned in Jerusalem, the whole religious system wanted to kill him. They accused him of polluting the holy place and preaching false doctrines. His life was in danger; even the soldiers "feared lest Paul be pulled to pieces." So they took him by force and locked him away in a castle. The next night the Lord Himself spoke to Paul, and what a word He brought: "Cheer up! There's even more trouble to come!"

The cost of following Christ was clear in the lives of these men of God—and if we are going to be like our Master, then we must embrace this cost as well. Enduring it becomes a joy because Jesus promises to stand with us in every situation. And we can face anything or anyone when we know the Lord stands with us.

So count the cost and know that your reward, in all things, is the precious presence of Jesus Christ.

∽ 12 ∽
WE WILL BE TESTED

Rest assured, those of us who want to walk righteously before the Lord are going to face trials. In fact, the deeper our walk with Christ, the more intense our furnace of testing will be. Scripture gives us the reason: It is because the Lord wants to burn out the impurities in our hearts and conform us into the image of His Son.

> "The people who know their God shall be strong, and carry out great exploits. And those of the people who understand shall instruct many; yet for many days they shall fall by sword and flame, by captivity and plundering. Now when they fall, they shall be aided with a little help. . . . And some of those of understanding shall fall, to refine them, purify them, and make them white, until the time of the end; because it is still for the appointed time."
>
> Daniel 11:32–35

This prophecy tells us that a great time of testing is coming upon "those of understanding." Just who are these people of understanding who will be tested? *They are the righteous*—those who do exploits for the Lord, who walk with God and have the wisdom of Christ.

You may find yourself in circumstances right now that cause you to wonder, "Why is my faith being tested? Why is all of this happening to me?"

It helps to understand why God allows these trials if you think back to your school days. When a test was given, your answers revealed how much you had actually learned of what you had been taught. In the New Testament, Paul speaks of a different school, one in which we are "learning Christ" and "have been taught by Him, as the truth is in Jesus" (Ephesians 4:20–21). If you belong to Jesus, you are in His school. You may have thought you had already graduated—but none of us will until we are in glory!

When I was in school, I hated pop quizzes, those annoying, unannounced tests. Yet the Lord has told us to be ready to be tested at any time—and that such tests will continue until Jesus returns. All who are hungry for more of Jesus will go through these fiery trials and be purged of all that is not Christlike in preparation for the soon-coming wedding of the Lamb.

This means we are not to run from the time of testing. Instead we are to be on our knees beseeching God that Christ be formed in us. We are to long in our souls to become real followers of God. We are to be *obsessed* with the desire to be a man or woman of God. Our hearts and lips should cry out, "Jesus, make me into Your own image. Let me become Your bond slave!"

There is one thing I want more than anything else in this world, and that is to become a true man of God. I want my living and my dying to bring glory to Jesus. Do you feel that way, too? Then we must all be prepared to enter His school.

I can't even begin to number all the ways the Lord tests His children, but there are four tests common to all of us, and I want to focus on them. But first I want to say a word to those who may be enduring hardship for another reason. These people are not facing tests of the Lord's choosing but, rather, are suffering from their own choices. One reason is sin and the other is wrong decisions.

If you want to hunger for Jesus but know you have sin in your life, then every occurrence of sin may feel like unexpected ocean waves sweeping over your soul, and you can't understand why you are swamped again. You cry out, "O God, it's too much for me. I can't handle it anymore." You are wounded knowing that you have spiritual corruption within, and it so sickens your mind that it has likely begun to affect your body. You are weighed down with depression and fear.

Know that because God loves you He will work to cleanse you. He brings His wrath and chastening upon obstinate wickedness. But it is a *loving* chastening upon those who repent and return to Him. You may feel God's arrows in your soul because of your past and present sins, but if you have a repentant heart and want to turn from error, you can call upon His chastening love. You will be corrected—but with His great mercy and compassion. You will not feel His wrath as the heathen do, but rather the rod of His discipline, applied by His loving hand.

Or perhaps your suffering comes from making wrong decisions. How many women are suffering because they married men whom God warned them not to marry? Now they are being abused and feel as if they are living in hell. How many children are breaking their parents' hearts, bringing them to the end of their ropes? Yet many times this happens because of the parents' own past years of sin, neglect and compromise.

You know you have arrived at your lowest point. It is time to seek the Lord in brokenness, repentance and faith. It is time to receive a new infusion of Holy Ghost strength. It is time to be renewed and refreshed, to have spiritual strength overflow within you.

You see, when you cry out to God, He pours His strength into you:

"In the day when I cried out, You answered me, and made me bold with strength in my soul. . . . Though I walk in the midst of trouble, You will revive me; You will stretch out Your hand against the wrath of my enemies, and Your right hand will save me. The Lord will perfect that which concerns me; Your mercy, O Lord, endures forever."

Psalm 138:3, 7–8

Let's assume now that we have cleansed our lives as much as we know how. We are not following paths of known sin, and we are trusting the Lord to work with us and through us in troubles that we may have brought on ourselves. It is not until we come to the end of ourselves that we throw ourselves completely on the Lord. Then we are ready to study in the school of the Holy Spirit. Here, then, are four tests that He may use to purify His children.

1. We are tested by afflictions—both our own and others'.

One of the most difficult things for Christians to accept is the suffering of the righteous. Up to the time of Christ, the Jews associated prosperity and good health with godliness. They believed that if you were wealthy, in good health or otherwise blessed, it was because God was showing that He was pleased with you. This was why Jesus' disciples had a hard time understanding His statement that "it is easier for a camel to go through the eye of a needle than for a rich man to enter the kingdom of God" (Matthew 19:24). The disciples asked, "Who then can be saved?"

Likewise today, there is an erroneous doctrine that says if you are in covenant with God you will never suffer; just call out to your covenant partner, God, and He will come running and solve everything immediately. But this is not the Gospel! The heroes of faith listed in Hebrews 11 all walked in covenant with God and they suffered stonings, mockings, torture and violent deaths (verses 36–38). Paul himself, who walked closely with God, was shipwrecked, stoned, whipped, left for dead, robbed, jailed and persecuted. He suffered the loss of all things. Why? These were all testings and purgings, the proving of his faith to the glory of God.

I don't know what your area of testing may be. I do know that many of God's precious ones have prayed for years for their deliverance, particularly physical healing, and are still waiting for it. I believe we will have afflictions and I believe in healing. But I also believe that God allows *healing afflictions.* David said, "Before I was afflicted I went astray, but now I keep Your word" (Psalm 119:67).

At times I've had to endure physical pain for years. Each time I've prayed for God to heal me, yet through the pain I could feel God working in my life, driving me to Jesus and keeping me on my knees. And after each painful episode passed I could say it had been good for me. Do you want to be a man or woman of God? Do you want the hand of God on your life? Then drink your cup of pain and bathe your bed in tears. Ask God not only for healing, but for what He wants you to learn from the trial.

Your pain may not be physical; sometimes another pain feels much worse. It's the pain of being bruised and rejected by friends, the pain that parents feel when teenagers trample their hearts and become strangers to them. It's the pain that fills the hearts of husbands and wives when walls of silence build up and first love disappears. How tragic it seems, the turmoil within, the difficulties at home, the restless, sleepless nights—knowing that God is real, that you're walking in the Spirit and loving Jesus with all that's in you, and yet you are still enduring affliction. I say to you, hold fast: God promises to deliver you.

The apostle Peter offered these encouraging words about our trials and testings:

Beloved, do not think it strange concerning the fiery trial which is to try you, as though some strange thing happened to you; but rejoice to the extent that you partake of Christ's sufferings, that when His glory is revealed, you may also be glad with exceeding joy.

1 Peter 4:12–13

Now for a little while, if need be, you have been grieved by various trials, that the genuineness of your faith, being much more precious than gold that perishes, though it is tested by fire, may be found to praise, honor, and glory at the revelation of Jesus Christ.

1 Peter 1:6–7

I believe that we will have to learn the lesson before the pain will be lifted. We enact this ourselves when we discipline our children. One of the worst things a parent can do to a child who is being disciplined is to offer sympathy, comfort and ease before the child learns the lesson. This can destroy the child! If the rod is spared and the lesson never learned, rebellion sets in. The child will believe that he can do something wrong and get away with it. It will affect not only his relationship with his parents, but will spread into every area—including his faith.

Jesus is our trustworthy parent, and while we are being disciplined we can call on Him as much as we want. But He will not move until we have learned what He wants to teach us. He will not allow destructive sin to take hold in our hearts—so He will not lift the rod until we yield.

Yet we mustn't forget that the whole time we're being tested and disciplined we are under God's protection. Peter says further that those who are tested by many trials and temptations are "kept by the power of God through faith" (1 Peter 1:5). You see, when Jesus allows suffering and trials in our lives, He's after one thing—the same thing He sought when He asked Abraham to sacrifice his beloved son Isaac. God allowed Abraham to lead Isaac all the way up the mountain and raise the knife above him. Only then did the Lord say, "Stop!" What was God after? Simply this: "Abraham, do I mean more to you than the object of your deepest earthly affections?" Abraham proved he was willing to lay down all that was near and dear to him—even the son who was the sole object of God's promise to him—and to put his future totally in God's hands. He gave his all to the Lord.

During this time of testing we do well to check our attitudes. Are our hearts still grateful to God for His love and mercy? Do we continue to praise His perfect goodness? Or do we murmur and complain that He has forgotten us, that He doesn't really care much about us?

Nothing will reveal the contents of our hearts like suffering. Take care that if a complaining spirit is exposed in you, you repent of it!

God hates murmuring and complaining. In fact, He allowed the children of Israel to suffer all kinds of hardships in the wilderness because the people had become habitual murmurers. Their hardships could be traced to their tongues!

They murmured because they had no water, so God gave them water from a rock. They complained because they had no bread, so God gave them bread from dew on the ground. Then they complained because they had no meat, so God gave them meat from out of the sky. The Lord gave them all these things and what was their reaction? The Bible says the people loathed it. They still complained once they got what they wanted!

There are Christians today who would complain about what they got if God answered their prayers because murmurers are never satisfied. If you do what they think you should do, they come up with a dozen more demands. The list never ends because their spirits are out of control—not under the governing power of the Holy Spirit. The Bible says of them, "These are grumblers, complainers, walking according to their own lusts" (Jude 16).

Murmuring begins in the thoughts—thoughts of discontent, of being mistreated by the Lord, of being misunderstood by God's people. Scripture warns us today, "Neither murmur ye, as some of them also murmured, and were destroyed of the destroyer" (1 Corinthians 10:10–11, kjv).

Another way we can be tested in this area of affliction is by witnessing the suffering of righteous, holy servants of God. This kind of testing is probably the most difficult to understand. We read in the Scriptures that "many are the afflictions of the righteous, but the Lord delivers him out of them all" (Psalm 34:19). Yet we see many devoted Christians dying before our eyes. Some suffer agonizing pain.

In truth, we should not be surprised when we see the godly suffer. Peter said, "Christ also suffered for us, leaving us an example, that you should follow His steps" (1 Peter 2:21), and, "Let those who suffer according to the will of God commit their souls to Him in doing good, as to a faithful Creator" (1 Peter 4:19). Jesus Himself said, "In the world you will have tribulation" (John 16:33). The

Greek word here for *tribulation* is *thlipsis*, meaning "anguish, burdens, persecution, trouble." Furthermore Jesus warned us about the difficulties of the last days: "They will deliver you up to tribulation and kill you, and you will be hated by all nations for My name's sake" (Matthew 24:9). Note that this says "all nations." Some think we are exempt from trouble in America because we are "getting back to God" by working to evangelize the world and supporting Israel.

My secretary's sister, Faith, spent her last 25 years helping ghetto children. She was a godly, caring, humble disciple of Jesus Christ who did everything He commanded her to do. Not long ago she died of bone cancer, and while I was praying for her just prior to her death, I felt Jesus take her by the right hand and lead her into calm, green pastures.

I know some are offended and confused at my saying this, but as David said, "Precious in the sight of the Lord is the death of His saints" (Psalm 116:15). *Precious* in Hebrew means "valuable, necessary." It means that He needs them, that their deaths are necessary to His eternal purposes. Paul said boldly, "Christ will be magnified in my body, whether by life or by death" (Philippians 1:20). He went on to say, "Stand fast . . . and not in any way terrified by your adversaries, which is to them a proof of perdition, but to you of salvation" (Philippians 1:27–28). Paul was telling us that even though suffering and death are signs to the world of loss, ruin or disaster, to those who know God they are deliverance.

I am convinced we don't understand the kind of marvelous deliverance the Lord has in mind for His children. His ways are far above ours. I've visited suffering believers in hospitals who had more faith and hope than all the Christians around them who were praying for healing. In some cases, the suffering ones usually ended up praying for the others. When you have that kind of hope in you, you're not living for this world anymore—you're living for eternity. Those who have suffered and died holding strongly to their faith have received a true healing; it has meant Christ for them. Peter said they "partake of Christ's sufferings, that when His glory is revealed, [they] may also be glad with exceeding joy" (1 Peter 4:13). Their faith, demonstrated here, will bring great honor to God *in glory.*

God wants to plant something in our hearts through all our testings and trials. He wants us to be able to say, "Lord Jesus, You're my Protector, and I believe You rule over the events of my life. If anything happens to me, it's only because You allowed it, and I trust Your purpose in doing it. Help me understand the lesson You want me to learn from it. If I walk in righteousness and have Your joy in my heart, then my living and dying will bring glory to You. I trust that You may have some prepared glory, some eternal purpose that my finite mind doesn't understand. But either way, I'll say, 'Jesus, whether I live or die, I am Yours!' "

2. We are tested by delayed answers to prayer.

Most of us pray as David did: "In the day that I call, answer me speedily" (Psalm 102:2). "I am in trouble; hear me speedily" (Psalm 69:17). The Hebrew word for *speedily* means "right now, hurry up, in the very hour I call on You, do it!" David was saying, "Lord, I put my trust in You—but please hurry!"

God is in no hurry. He doesn't jump at our commands. In fact, at times you may wonder if He will ever answer. You cry out, weep, fast and hope—but days go by, weeks, months, even years, and you don't receive even the slightest evidence that God is hearing you. First you question yourself: "Something must be blocking my prayers, some hidden sin. Maybe I asked amiss. Or perhaps my faith is too weak." You become perplexed, and over time your attitude toward God becomes something like this: "Lord, what do I have to do to get this prayer answered? You promised in Your Word to give me an answer, and I prayed in faith. How many tears must I shed?"

Why does God delay answers to sincere prayers? It certainly isn't because He lacks power. He could merely wink an eye or think a thought and His work would be finished. And He is most willing —even more than we are—for us to receive from Him. No, the answer is found rather in this verse: "He spoke a parable to them, that men always ought to pray and not lose heart" (Luke 18:1).

The Greek word for *lose heart,* or *faint* in the King James Version, means "relax, become weak or weary in faith, give up the struggle, no longer wait for completion." Galatians 6:9 says, "Let us not grow weary while doing good, for in due season we shall reap if we do not lose heart." The Lord is seeking for a praying people who will not relax or grow weary of coming to Him. These people will wait on the Lord, not giving up before His work is completed. And they will be found waiting when He brings the answer.

I thought I had unshakable faith, that I fully trusted in the Lord. Then some of my very important prayers were not answered for a long time; in fact, some still are not answered. I reasoned with the Lord, "If You will just answer my prayers, it will build up my faith. I can go to the sanctuary and boast of Your faithfulness the way David did. Think of how others will be greatly encouraged." But the whole time the Lord was saying to me, *I don't build your faith on My answers—I build your faith on My delays!*

Anybody can believe when the answers to prayer are flooding in. But who's going to believe after a year or two years? As time goes on, we abandon our prayers and the belief that He will answer, and we move on to something else. We say to God, "I'll be faithful to You. But don't expect me to have faith to wait for answers to prayers anymore." In reality, God wants only to make sure you're not going to relax in your prayer vigil. He wants your heart set on persevering, no matter how long His answer takes.

Jesus gave us a parable to prove that He waits on us to dig in and determine not to give up. It is the parable of the distressed widow who kept coming to the judge seeking justice (see Luke 18:2–8). The judge finally granted her request only because he was worn down by her constant pleading: "Because this widow troubles me I will avenge her, lest by her continual coming she weary me" (verse 5). Jesus added to this parable, "And shall God not avenge His own elect who cry out day and night to Him, though He bears long with them? I tell you that He will avenge them speedily" (verses 7–8).

You say, "But doesn't Jesus seem to be speaking a paradox in this verse? First He says God 'bears long' with us—then He says He 'will avenge us speedily.'" Most of us misinterpret this passage completely. You see, Jesus isn't speaking of delaying a long time. He says God *wants* to answer us speedily but is *enduring* something.

God is bearing something that calls for patience on His part. He's saying, *I'll put up with this thing I see in your heart—I'll bear with you—until you're willing to lay hold of Me for the answer as I desire you should.*

As I look back at some of the things I've prayed for over a long period, I hear the Lord saying, *David, I'm holding up this request to you, like a mirror. And through this, I'm going to show you what's deep in your heart.* What I've seen reflected in that mirror are doubt . . . fear . . . unbelief . . . things that have made me throw myself at Jesus' feet and cry, "O Lord! I'm not interested in the answer anymore, but only in getting this spirit out of me. I don't want to doubt You—to pray and weep for an answer, yet still have seeds of unbelief in my heart!"

It's true that the hardest part of faith is the last half hour. When it looks as if God won't answer, we give up, putting all behind us and going on to something else. And as we do this, we think we are surrendering to God's providence, His sovereign will. We say, "Lord, do what You think is best," or, "Well, God, You must not have wanted it after all." That is *not* what God ever intended! When we pray for what is obviously the will of God—salvation of a family member, for instance—we have every right to hold on and never give up until Jesus answers. We have every reason not to listen to the devil. And we have every right to ask God to plant the faith of Jesus Christ in us and not let us relax until we see completion.

Too often, instead, we faint—we fail the test. If we hadn't fainted, we would still be holding on more determined than ever to see the answer through. Yet the Lord sees our fainting heart all along. In fact, He gives us a picture of this humbling experience in 2 Kings 6–7.

Samaria was under seige by Ben-Hadad and his great Syrian army. The city was starving: A donkey's head sold for eighty pieces of silver, a pint of dove's dung for five. The prophet Elisha had prophesied to the king of Samaria that God was going to deliver the people supernaturally. He said to hold on—to wait, pray, repent and trust God no matter how bad things got.

As the king paced atop the city walls, he may have thought,

"How long must this go on? We can't hold out much longer. If God doesn't answer soon, we'll have to go out with the white flag and surrender." Then a woman saw the king and cried out, "Yesterday my neighbor and I boiled and ate my baby. We agreed that today we would eat her baby, but now she has hidden her child. King, it's unfair—make her give up her baby, too!"

That did it! The king ripped open his sackcloth, and in a rage he bellowed, "Elisha, off comes your head! You had us believing that God would answer your prayer. You told us a miracle would happen." When the king found Elisha praying among the elders, he screamed, "Why should I wait for the Lord any longer?" In other words, "It's too late! The deadline has come and gone and God didn't keep His word. Prayer isn't going to help. It's time to take matters into our own hands!"

While the king was fainting—quitting on his faith—the answer was almost at the gate. Elisha told him, "Tomorrow about this time a seah [about eight gallons] of fine flour shall be sold for a shekel, and two seahs of barley for a shekel, at the gate of Samaria" (2 Kings 7:1). It's too bad the king hadn't waited another 24 hours before blowing up. He didn't know that God was at work creating a miracle. In the Syrian camp, a miraculous buzzing filled the air—the sound of a huge army of chariots rumbling toward them. Panic swept over the Syrians, and they dropped everything and ran for their lives. So the Samarians brought home wagonloads of the Syrians' food. Vegetables, fine flour and barrels of barley poured through the city gates. Watching this, the king must have been red-faced as he recalled stating, "God didn't keep His word!"

This kind of thing must have happened to me at least a dozen times. I've given up and said, "Oh, well, this must not have been God's will. It's an impossible situation." And sometimes the answer came within an hour of my words! Is that what's happening with you? Have you given up and stopped pressing in? You must recognize that God is already at work, and His answer is just about to arrive. It is when we wait in faith and see it through that we grow in faith and bring greater glory to His name.

3. We are tested by our failings.

In saying this, I do not mean that Christians who fall back into old sins and turn back to the world are being tested. No, those believers are being *shipwrecked.* Peter sends this warning to believers who are growing in holiness and are set on following the Lord: "Beware lest you also fall from your own steadfastness, being led away with the error of the wicked" (2 Peter 3:17).

We are tested by our failings when we take a fall in spite of all the progress we've made with the Lord. A number of things could be the cause of that fall—a root of anger, for instance. If you asked someone what caused his fall into anger, he might answer with something like this: "I was provoked by my own family and I blew up. I can't understand it—I thought I was becoming a little sweeter, a little more like Jesus. But somebody pushed the wrong button and I lost it!"

If there is a root of anger or bitterness or pride or any other area God is working on in our lives, He will make our homes a testing ground. We will be provoked time after time until all of the hidden fault is exposed and plucked out by the Holy Spirit.

We may think, *I'm only human. How much am I supposed to take?* It does not matter that we are provoked, or even that we might be in the right. The provoking simply proves we need deliverance in that area. Scripture says: "Let *all* bitterness, wrath, anger, clamor [fighting], and evil speaking be put away from you, with all malice [grudges]" (Ephesians 4:31). God's going to keep testing us until we say, "I've got a spirit in me that's got to go!" We will see no growth in Christ, no peace at home or on the job, until we can say, "You're right, Lord—take it out!"

Sometimes when we are tested we may tend to feel unworthy. We may even wonder if the Lord still loves us. Let me assure you that if we have truly repented God puts His loving arms around each of us and says, "I allowed that to happen so you could see what's in your heart. But you're making progress, real growth in areas that matter to Me. You've said you want to walk with Me, and I'm teaching you. I know what's inside of you, and I'll allow you to be provoked until you get rid of it all. But the important thing is, I'm here with you. I'll stand with you in the midst of all your trials!"

Our response is: "Lord, You've put Your finger on some areas in me. Pluck them out of my heart. Encourage me, Lord, that I'm not going backward—instead, I'm going forward with You."

4. The test of isolation.

I know what it is like to face divine silence, not to hear God's voice for a season. I have walked through periods of total confusion with no apparent guidance, the still, small voice behind me completely silent. There were times when I had no friend nearby to satisfy my heart with a word of advice. All my patterns of guidance from before had gone awry, and I was left in total darkness. I could not see my way, and I made mistake after mistake. I wanted to say, "O God, what has happened? I don't know which way to go!"

That's some positive confession to make, you may say! But all of us will face that kind of confusion when God begins to test our commitment to Him. Thank God, it is only "the dark night of the soul," and it will pass because the Lord desires to make our paths clear. The following words came from the lips of Jesus, God's own Son: "My God, My God, why have You forsaken Me?" (Matthew 27:46).

The hour of isolation comes when it appears God has hidden His face, and none of your friends truly understands what you are going through. But, you ask, does God really hide His face from those He loves? Isn't it possible He lifts His hand for a short while to teach us trust and dependence? The Bible answers clearly: "God withdrew from [Hezekiah], in order to test him, that He might know all that was in his heart" (2 Chronicles 32:31).

I can honestly say that Jesus has never been more real to me than He is today. But I can also say that there are times it seems you can do little to break through to heaven—times when you get on your knees and discover that the heavens are as brass. Prayer doesn't break through. You feel nothing but emptiness and defeat. And your heart cries out, "O God, where are You?"

God says, "With a little wrath I hid My face from you for a moment" (Isaiah 54:8). But also it is He "who redeems your life from destruction, who crowns you with lovingkindness and tender mercies" (Psalm 103:4). He promises He will extend tender, loving mercies in our times of isolation.

One time, after one of my evangelistic meetings in San Francisco, a certain young man walked into the prayer room. I had met him years before when he had attended one of my crusades, and he had cried in repentance and prayed for salvation. That night he had walked out of the prayer room with true joy in his heart. But now he looked totally forlorn; I had never seen such a sad young face in all my life. He said, "Mr. Wilkerson, I don't know which way to turn. I have no joy, and God seems to be far away. I'm being tempted, and I'm afraid I'm going to backslide and lose my touch of God. I feel nothing but fear and trembling!"

I put my hand on the young man's shoulder and said, "Son, this is your hour of trial. God is testing you to see what is in your heart. Will you repent, accept His forgiveness and keep coming to the Light? God has not forsaken you."

Suddenly tears began streaming down his cheeks. "You mean God really isn't mad at me after all?"

"No," I answered.

Then he asked, "Is my restlessness and despair the result of some terrible habit in my life?" I told him only he could answer that. He replied, "No, I don't think so."

Then suddenly he began to see the light: It was not God's fault after all! It was his own neglect of prayer and hunger for the Word during his season of suffering that caused him to fear and stumble. At that moment, the Spirit of the Lord began to minister hope to him, and he raised his hands and praised the Lord: "Take me through, Lord. Restore my faith!" When I left him, he was thanking God for bringing him back to a solid commitment. The Holy Spirit was beginning to shine forth in him again.

I've known what it means to pray for, and then receive, the finances needed to sustain our ministry. I've known what it means to walk for a whole year with Jesus leading me every step of the way, His voice behind me saying, *David, this is the way, walk in it.* I've known what it means to get out a pad and a pencil and to write down questions and have Him answer them for me. Then I've immediately turned around to face nights of deep, dark confusion when I didn't know which way to turn. I've made multiple mistakes that cast me down in despair, and I've cried out, "O God, where are You?" I've gone into my prayer closet for three or four weeks at a time and said, "God, I've got to touch You. I've got to be broken." And I've felt nothing but my own grief, coldness of heart and the heavy silence of heaven. Yet through it all I sensed God was at work. *Just hold steady,* I've heard the Spirit say. *Ride out your storm. When the enemy shall come in like a flood, the Spirit of the Lord shall lift up a standard against him* (see Isaiah 59:19).

Know Whom You Have Believed

You may be going through a flood of trials right now. You know what I'm talking about when I say the heavens are as brass. You know all about repeated failures. You've waited and waited for answers to prayer. You've been served a cup of affliction. Nothing and nobody can touch that need in your heart!

A woman came up to me once after I preached about testing and trials. She said, "When I came to church this morning, I walked in acting happy and carefree. But when you talked about the cup of pain I began to weep. I realized I was just putting up a front. My husband has left me and my home is in turmoil. I've had to cover it all up. But now I know—I'm being flooded!" That woman was broken before the Lord. I prayed with her for God to keep her faith strong, and she left with the true joy of the Lord in her heart.

When a man or woman is hungering for God, enemy forces will come against that person with great fury. In fact, there is also a difficult time of sifting for God's children. But that believer can stand up and say, "Though I am tried and tested, though all these forces are arrayed against me, 'I know whom I have believed and am persuaded that He is able to keep what I have committed to Him until that Day' " (2 Timothy 1:12).

That's the time to take your stand! You don't have to be able to laugh or rejoice, because you may not have any happiness at the

147

moment. In fact, you may have nothing but turmoil in your soul. But you can know God is still with you, because Scripture says, "The Lord sitteth upon the flood; yea, the Lord sitteth King forever" (Psalm 29:10, KJV).

Soon you will hear His voice: *Don't get excited, don't panic. Just keep your eyes on Me. Commit all things to Me.* And you will know that you remain the object of His incredible love.

～ 13 ～
SIFTED SAINTS

"You are those who have continued with Me in My trials. And I bestow upon you a kingdom, just as My Father bestowed one upon Me, that you may eat and drink at My table in My kingdom, and sit on thrones judging the twelve tribes of Israel."

And the Lord said, "Simon, Simon! Indeed, Satan has asked for you, that he may sift you as wheat. But I have prayed for you, that your faith should not fail; and when you have returned to Me, strengthen your brethren."

But he said to Him, "Lord, I am ready to go with You, both to prison and to death."

Then He said, "I tell you, Peter, the rooster shall not crow this day before you will deny three times that you know Me."

Luke 22:28–34

You may have heard of the late Kathryn Kuhlman, a healing minister from Pittsburgh who was used mightily by God. The Lord graciously allowed me to minister with her in that city for more than five years, and during that time my wife, Gwen, and I got to know her well.

One thing I remember very clearly about Kathryn was the hushed tone of voice she used whenever we discussed Satan and the powers of darkness. On one occasion I began telling her about our work with drug addicts and alcoholics in New York City. She must have thought I was being too nonchalant about the subject as it related to demonic activity, because as I spoke she became very somber. Finally, in a quiet voice she told me, "David, don't ever take lightly the subject of spiritual battles or satanic powers. It's a sobering topic."

To my knowledge, Kathryn never once feared Satan or demons. But the subject of principalities and powers of darkness was no light matter to her. God had given her spiritual eyes to see just a portion of the war being waged in the heavenlies for the souls of men and women.

When Jesus walked the earth, He knew all too well the fierceness of Satan's power, that he comes with every weapon in hell to sift the Lord's people. I don't think any of us can comprehend the great conflict raging right now in the spirit realm. Nor do we realize how determined Satan is to destroy all believers who have fixed their hungering hearts firmly on going all the way with Christ. But it is true that in our Christian walk, we cross a line—the "obedience line" I talked about earlier in the story of Ruth—that sets off every alarm in hell. And the moment we cross that line into a life of obedience to God's Word and dependence on Jesus alone, we become a threat to the kingdom of darkness and a prime target of demonic principalities and powers. The testimony of every believer who turns to the Lord with all his heart includes the sudden onslaught of strange and intense troubles and trials.

If you've crossed the obedience line, then you're making waves in the unseen world. We've all experienced harassment from hell of some kind.

The congregation of Times Square Church, located in the midtown section of the largest city in the U.S., represent the broadest cross section of people, all of whom experience this kind of harassment. One Sunday night I had to interrupt the worship to make this announcement: "Someone is trying to break into a yellow Mercedes parked right outside the door. If this car is yours, get out there quickly!" Thieves had already stolen the radio and were in the process of stealing the car. Thank the Lord they ran away and the car was rescued.

The owner turned out to be a woman very committed to the Lord's work. Later that week she called my office and said, "Pastor, I knew immediately that was harassment from Satan. He was trying to keep me from hearing the Gospel preached. But I won't be put off!"

Another woman from New Jersey had her car fender damaged, and on another occasion her car was stolen. I knew what was happening in that situation: This woman also was changing and growing in the Lord. She had crossed the line for Jesus and now Satan was bullying her, trying to discourage her from coming to church.

"Simon, Simon! . . . Satan has asked for you, that he may sift you as wheat." Here Jesus introduces this subject of the sifting of saints. In Christ's day, grain workers used a sieve just before they sacked grain. They shoveled wheat into a square box covered with netting, then turned the box upside down and shook it violently. The grit and dirt fell through the netting until only the grain kernels remained.

Sift in this verse means to be shaken and separated—to be shocked through the agitation of sudden trials. Jesus used this analogy to say to Peter: "Satan believes you're nothing but grit and dirt, and that when he puts you in the sieve and shakes you, you will fall through to the ground!"

There are tests and trials, and then there is *sifting*. I see sifting as one major, all-out satanic onslaught. It is usually compressed into a short but very intense period of time. For Jesus it was forty days and forty nights in the wilderness, as Satan came at Him with every deception from the kingdom of darkness. For Peter, the sifting would last only a few days. But those days would become the most faith-shaking, shocking and remorseful days of his life.

Note that Jesus did not pray Peter would be spared from Satan's sifting. Rather, He prayed that his faith would not fail. That is Satan's prime target: our faith. Let's study this example as it relates to our faith, and the sifting of our lives by the devil.

When Sifting Comes

We learn first from this story that Peter's sifting came *immediately after a great revelation.*

Peter and the other disciples had just received from Jesus a promise of fruitful ministry. "I bestow upon you a kingdom," He had said, that they might eat and drink at His table and sit on thrones judging the twelve tribes of Israel.

The Greek word for *bestow* is taken from a root word meaning "to channel." Jesus had made an incredible promise to His disciples. In essence He told them, "I am going to channel My Kingdom through you, just as the Father made Me a channel of His glory." Not only would these men be channels of Christ's majesty, but they also would be seated at the Lord's table to enjoy eternal intimacy with Him. They would become princes, ruling and reigning with Him!

Yet little did Peter know that while Jesus spoke of these glorious promises, His heart was praying in agony over what He saw in the invisible spirit world. Satan was at the Father's throne, accusing Peter and asking permission to get his hands on him, as he had done with Job. He must have said something like this: "The Son of God calls this man Peter 'Rock,' saying He will build a Church on his kind of faith. I say he is not a rock of faith—he is chaff and unworthy to be a channel of Your glory! Let me shake him, let me put him to the test. He has an evil streak, he won't last. He's going to fall!"

You must understand that Satan seeks to sift only those who threaten his work. He goes after the tree with the most potential to bear fruit. But why did the devil desire to sift Peter now? Why was he so anxious to test him? Well, for three years Peter had been casting out devils and healing the sick. And Satan had heard Jesus promise the disciples another baptism, one of Holy Ghost power and fire—and he trembled! Now, the devil heard God's ultimate plan for Peter to rule in the new Kingdom. He realized that the past three years would be nothing compared to the greater works Peter and the other disciples would perform as a prelude to that day. Having already pulled down Judas, he would have to look for a measure of corruption in Peter to build on, to make Peter's faith fail.

Perhaps, like Peter, you are in the sieve right now, being shaken and sifted. But, you ask, why me? And why now? First of all, you ought to rejoice that you have such a reputation in hell! Satan never would have asked God's permission to sift you unless you had crossed the line of obedience. Why else would he spend his efforts harassing and troubling you, scaring you and shaking all that you have? He is sifting you because you play an important part in God's Church in these last days. God is doing a new thing once again in this last, great revival, and you have been set apart by Him to be a powerful witness to many. He has set you free, and is preparing you for His eternal purposes. And the greater your gifts, the greater your potential, the greater your surrender to the will of God—the more severe your sifting will be.

Sifting Can Remove Pride

Peter was not aware of any glaring weaknesses in himself. Listen to his testimony: "Lord, I'm ready to go with You! I've had three wonderful years of the best training possible. I've been around. I have experience. I've seen demons run, and I've moved crowds toward God. I've grown so much! I'm not the man I was three years ago. Praise God, I'm ready, and I'm going all the way with You."

Even the Lord's warning could not shake Peter's self-confidence. Jesus was trying to shake the disciple, to wake him up to the danger just ahead, but it seems Peter did not hear a word of it. It made no impression on him because he had no discernment. Peter was in grave danger, only hours away from committing an unbelievable sin. Yet he went confidently on his way, boasting, "I'm ready—I won't fail. If anybody is going all the way, it is I!"

Perhaps you, too, have been in Peter's shoes at times. God has His hand on you, you've grown in the Lord and you love Him with all your heart—but you don't think you can fall. You're not aware that Satan is about to sift you, that you're going to be hit heavily by the enemy's assault.

One example of this comes immediately to my mind—that of a powerful young evangelist who was greatly used of God to heal the sick. He had a special anointing and received revelation in the Word. God's hand was heavy upon him.

Then he and his wife began drifting apart and they separated. About that time, the evangelist's eye fell on a young woman. He knew it was wrong to pursue her, so he decided to be "just a friend." He began calling her two or three times a day and every night, "just talking about Jesus," he said. Eventually he ended up divorcing his wife and marrying the other woman.

Yes, he still has his ministry, but it is only a fraction of what it was meant to be. We mustn't be deceived: This man missed God. His example should serve as a sober warning to all of us. May God drive out all spiritual pride from our hearts, and may we heed His warnings.

As for Peter, within 24 hours of his boasting he became a moral cripple—cursing, carried away by cowardice and denying Christ three times. He did something so evil and wicked he never could have thought it possible. Yet Jesus could not—and would not—stop the sifting process for Peter. There was something inside this disciple that three years of pure teaching could not touch, that miracles, signs and wonders could not shake, that Christ's warnings could not dig out. The only thing left for Jesus to do was to let Peter go into the fire, straight into the hands of Satan and overwhelming temptation.

Peter had to be broken and humbled. He had to see the pride lurking in his heart. Whenever such a lack of discernment and blindness toward self-confidence exist, the sifting hand of Satan is the only alternative left to cleanse the vessel for Christ's use.

The Role of Prayer

When someone is going through the fire of sifting, what should those around him do? What did Jesus do about Peter's imminent fall? Jesus said, "I have prayed for you, that your faith not fail."

I look at this wonderful example of Christ's love and realize I know almost nothing about how to love those who fall. Surely Jesus is that "friend who sticks closer than a brother" (Proverbs 18:24). He saw both the good and the bad in Peter and concluded, "This man is worth saving. Satan desires him, but I desire him all the more." Judas could not be saved; he had no heart for the Lord. He was sold out to greed and covetousness and that became an open door for Satan. But Peter truly loved the Lord, and Jesus told him, "I have prayed for you." Jesus had seen this coming for a long time. He had probably spent many hours before His Father talking about Peter—how He loved him, how needed Peter was in God's Kingdom, how He valued him as a friend.

Lord, give all of us that kind of love! When we see brothers and sisters compromising or heading for trouble or disaster, let us love them enough to warn them as firmly as Jesus warned Peter. Then we'll be able to say, "I am praying for you."

And we need to say this in love, not in an accusing way. Too often we react with, "You are so bad, so compromised. You need all the prayer you can get!" Or, "I'm going to pray for you. You sure need it." But Jesus did not lecture Peter. He did not say, "If only you'd listened. If only you'd stayed awake and prayed with Me in the Garden. If only you weren't so proud." Rather, Jesus said simply, "I have prayed for you." We, too, must take these brothers and sisters to God's throne and plead for them to come through these trials with their faith intact. And may they respond in kind when we find ourselves in the same situation.

In the original Greek, *you* is plural, meaning "all of you." Jesus was speaking about praying not only for Peter but for all the disciples—and for us today:

"I pray for them. I do not pray for the world but for those whom You have given Me, for they are Yours. . . . Holy Father, keep through Your name those whom You have given Me. . . . I do not pray that You should take them out of the world, but that You should keep them from the evil one."

John 17:9, 11, 15

When Jesus was confronted with the devil's schemes in the wilderness, He overcame them with God's Word: "It is written, 'Man shall not live by bread alone, but by every word that proceeds from the mouth of God' " (Matthew 4:4). "It is written again, 'You shall not tempt the Lord your God' " (Matthew 4:7). "Away with you, Satan! For it is written, 'You shall worship the Lord your God, and Him only you shall serve' " (Matthew 4:10).

Today we have yet another "It is written" with which we can do battle against Satan. It is this: "I have prayed for you, that your faith should not fail." You can tell the devil: "You may have gotten permission to sift me, to try to tear down my faith. But you need to know this: My Jesus is praying for me!"

After the Sifting

When Peter was sifted he failed miserably—*but not in his faith.* You may be thinking, "How can that be? This man denied knowing Jesus three different times. He cursed and swore it!"

But you see, if Peter failed, then Jesus' praying would have been to no avail. I know Peter's faith did not fail because just as he swore and it looked as if the Lord had lost a friend and an anointed disciple, Peter looked into the eyes of Jesus—and melted. He remembered how the Lord had said, "You will deny Me three times," and "Peter went out and wept bitterly" (Luke 22:61–62). *Wept bitterly* in the Greek actually means he cried "a piercing, violent cry." I picture Peter walking toward the Judean hills, falling on his face with hands outstretched, crying, "O Father, He was so right! I did not listen. He warned me that Satan would attempt to destroy my faith. I'm *not* ready! Die for Jesus? Why, I couldn't even stand up to a maid. Forgive me, O Lord—I love Him. To whom else shall I go?" Eventually Peter's faith grabbed hold of something else Jesus had said: "When you have returned to Me, strengthen your brethren" (Luke 22:32). How many times Peter must have played this over and over in his mind, pondering, "Didn't Jesus say I would return to Him, be brought back? Didn't He say I still had a ministry? After what I did, can I really help others?"

Yes, God answered His Son's prayer. And I can see Peter standing up with the Spirit of God flowing through him, his hands raised to the sky, shouting, "Satan, be gone! I failed Him, but I still love Him. He promised—in fact, He prophesied—that I would come back and be a strength to others, a rock. I'm going back to my brothers and sisters!" Indeed, Peter was the first disciple to reach the tomb when they were told Jesus had risen. He was with the other disciples when Jesus later appeared in their midst. He was there worshiping when Jesus was translated to glory. And it was Peter who stood as God's spokesman on the day of Pentecost—and what a sermon he preached!

A flood of new converts is coming back to the Lord today, Jews and Gentiles alike, and many backsliders as well. Where will they find strength in the troubled times ahead? From the returning, *sifted* saints, who can say with authority, "Don't trust yourself. Take heed when you think you stand, lest you fall" (see 1 Corinthians 10:12).

Do you sense a seductive pull of temptation in your life? Does some kind of deep trouble brew now in your heart? Then hear the words of Jesus and realize that Satan may have been given permission to sift you. Don't take it lightly. You don't have to fail as Peter did; in fact, we are to read his story and be warned by it. But even if you have failed and grieved the Lord Jesus, you can look into His face as Peter did and remember He is praying for you. Repent, return and then share your experience with others who are being sifted.

I have asked the Lord to help me give the same word of hope to fallen believers as Jesus did. He did not say, "*If* you come back," or, "*If* you are converted," but, "*When* you return." I want to be able to look at weeping, broken, failing sheep and say with hope and confidence, "When this sifting is over, when your faith is stronger, when you are restored—God will use you!"

So if you are one of God's "sifted saints," take heart. I know, and you must remember as well: Satan wouldn't come against you unless he had seen a glimpse of holiness and obedience in your heart.

~~ 14 ~~
THE SCHOOL OF SYMPATHY

A doctor friend once told me the process God used to enlist him in the school of sympathy. Doctors see so much pain that often they become immune to it, and at one time my friend was no different. He had very little empathy for people who suffered. He couldn't understand, for instance, why patients with kidney stones screamed in agony. *It can't be that bad,* he thought. *They must be acting just a little—perhaps to get medication.* Then one day he woke up with kidney stones of his own and the pain was worse than his patients had said. It was terrible! He needed painkillers just to get through the day. Today my friend has true sympathy for his patients' pain.

My wife has shared with me some of the letters she has received from women who have had mastectomies or gone for checkups because of a lump on their breasts. They know Gwen has survived many cancer operations, and that she knows the agony of waking up with terrible feelings of disfigurement. The women who write to Gwen are crying out for sympathy and hope, and my wife guards their letters like gold. These hurting women are like suffering students to her. She has gone through God's school of sympathy, and now she can offer comfort, hope and strength to them.

Likewise, today there is a Holy Ghost "school of sympathy," which consists of tested and sifted saints. They have been tossed to and fro, tempted, tried, mistreated. The Bible speaks of a "fellowship of His sufferings" (Philippians 3:10). It is a fellowship with Jesus, a sharing of deep, mysterious, unfathomable trials. For He, too, suffered great mental and physical anguish. Jesus was rejected, distrusted, abused, mocked and laughed at. He was lonely, hungry, poor, unloved, slandered, put to shame and made the butt of jokes. He was called a liar, a fraud, a false prophet. He was humiliated by others. His family misunderstood Him. His most trusted friends lost faith in Him. His own disciples forsook Him and fled. Finally Jesus was spat upon, mocked and murdered. Yes, Jesus sympathizes with all our hurts and sufferings because He went through them all Himself: "For we do not have a high priest who cannot sympathize with our weaknesses, but one who has been tempted in all things as we are, yet without sin" (Hebrews 4:15, NASB).

You can be sure that God has a divine purpose behind every single trial you are now enduring. And ultimately, I believe, it is to raise up comforters in the Body of Christ.

Suffering Produces Comforters

You may not understand why you have gone through such deep testings. In fact, life may have been so difficult for you at times that you nearly gave up. But then the Holy Spirit came and brought peace to your heart.

As our Comforter He comes to us in our deepest sorrow, and He strengthens and helps us and lifts our spirits. And there is eternal purpose behind His work: "That we may be able to comfort those who are in any trouble, with the comfort with which we ourselves are comforted by God. For as the sufferings of Christ abound in us, so our consolation also abounds through Christ" (2 Corinthians 1:4–5). Paul makes it clear that some people are permitted to endure much affliction, not just for their own learning but to benefit and teach others: "If we are afflicted, it is for your comfort and salvation" (2 Corinthians 1:6–7, NASB).

Who among us, though, can look at what he or she is going through and say, "This is going to comfort, bless and save others who will go through the same thing"? Hardly anyone! While it's hard to believe and accept during the time of trial, God's Word nevertheless holds true: "Tribulation produces perseverance" (Romans 5:3).

Through His school of suffering, God is training sympathizers. He sees the great tribulations that lie ahead for the Church— incredible sufferings and grievous persecutions. And God will not leave His people without tried and true witnesses in this last time. You have been in the Holy Ghost's school of sympathy because God has a ministry of comfort for you. You are being taught great lessons, all for the purpose of giving hope and consolation to others who only now are going into the fire.

The Body of Christ today needs a people who have not been offended or destroyed by their sufferings, who are not cast down, dejected or full of questions, but who instead hold fast to God's love, proving Him faithful in all things. They must be patient, enduring and strong in faith. They should be an example to the weak, a source of true comfort and consolation. It is easy for those who haven't suffered to throw around words of advice. But unless they have gone into the fire and died to their own wisdom and doctrines, their words are dead. They have no true comfort to offer those who truly need it.

We Have a Choice

Our sufferings will either train us or destroy us. Look at this description from Hebrews:

"For whom the Lord loves He chastens, and scourges every son whom He receives." If you endure chastening, God deals with you as with sons; for what son is there whom a father does not chasten?

But if you are without chastening, of which all have become partakers, then you are illegitimate and not sons. Furthermore, we have had human fathers who corrected us, and we paid them respect. Shall we not much more readily be in subjection to the Father of spirits and live? For they indeed for a few days chastened us as seemed best to them, but He for our profit, that we may be partakers of His holiness.

Now no chastening seems to be joyful for the present, but painful; nevertheless, afterward it yields the peaceable fruit of righteousness to those who have been trained by it.

Therefore, strengthen the hands which hang down, and the feeble knees, and make straight paths for your feet, so that what is lame may not be dislocated but rather be healed. Pursue peace with all people, and holiness, without which no one will see the Lord: looking carefully lest anyone fall short of the grace of God; lest any root of bitterness springing up cause trouble, and by this many become defiled.

Hebrews 12:6–15

It's all up to us. Still we can either allow our suffering to become a school of sympathy to help others, or else it will become a death camp that will destroy us and defile others who look up to us.

If we endure great sufferings because we are being chastened by the Lord, we can be comforted in knowing that He chastises us in great love, to produce His holiness in us. He says it is for our profit, and that if we are willing to be trained by it, afterward it will produce in us the peaceable fruit of righteousness.

If a seed of bitterness takes root, on the other hand, it will destroy and defile us. Yet there is a sure way to stop that root and defilement: Encourage ourselves in the Lord! Lift up limp hands, strengthen feeble knees and make straight paths for our feet, so that what is lame may be healed. This is a call to rouse ourselves, to shake off apathy, to get back to serving and trusting God, to be healed of doubt. We must rid ourselves of every thought of quitting. We must take captive every thought of "easing off," in total obedience to the Lord.

Afflictions or sufferings do not in themselves teach us. Many good people have learned nothing in their troubles; some have even lost ground with God. We can profit only through sufferings *understood* and afflictions *accepted* as from His hand. Our flesh is irritated and depressed by any kind of suffering and affliction. That's why so many false doctrines abound today, telling us Christians should never suffer (or even die!). These cater to the flesh. So unless we understand that God permits our sufferings and has a training purpose in all our afflictions, our spiritual growth will be hindered by these trials. David said, "In the day of my trouble I sought the Lord" (Psalm 77:2). And that is God's purpose—to break us from the love of this world and drive us to Jesus in total dependence for all our help.

God knows us! He permits our afflictions, saying, "You are the kind who forgets Me in good times. You neglect Me when all is well. But I love you too much to lose you to the devil. I'll awaken you through affliction, to remind you of how short life is and to make you dependent on Me."

Here are some good arguments to use when the devil tells you godly people don't suffer:

1. Christ suffered in the flesh mightily—and He was perfect.
2. Paul and all our Church fathers suffered great afflictions, yet God loved them dearly and used them mightily.
3. To the godly, suffering is not a sign of God's displeasure but a sign of sonship. Whom He loves, He chastens.
4. Every affliction is intended for my spiritual benefit and growth, and to equip me to sympathize with others in need.
5. My suffering may be grievous and painful. But if I'll accept it, afterward it will bear the fruit of holiness and pure love for God.

Deliverance Day

We looked earlier at this verse: "Many are the afflictions of the righteous" (Psalm 34:19). The Hebrew word used in this passage for "afflictions" is *ra,* which means "evil, calamity, distress, mischief, sorrow, trouble, wretchedness." That covers just about everything that could happen to a human being. These afflictions are many—

and, yes, they do happen to the righteous. That is God's Word, plain and simple.

But Scripture also says, "The righteous cry out, and the Lord hears, and delivers them out of all their troubles" (Psalm 34:17). *Deliver* means "snatch away, pull out, rescue."

How are we to understand deliverance in this sense when a trial can seem unending? Certainly no one doubts that God can intervene and stop all our suffering, pain or distress. By simply speaking a word He can send a legion of angels, a host from heaven to our aid. (We already know He has angels encamped about each one of us who believes.) But we also know that like a good father who disciplines his children, an all-wise God would not put us in the furnace to purify us, then stop halfway through His refining process and let us off the hook because He felt sorry for us. He would not quit on us before He accomplished His will; then it all would have been in vain!

You see, we are not always delivered by the easing of our sufferings, but rather by the intensification of them because God wants to hasten our escape through our dying to this world. We are delivered not when we are freed from suffering, *but when we die to our flesh!* Have you cried out to God for deliverance and then watched as your troubles increased? Are things getting worse for you now and not better? Then rejoice, because you are about to be delivered up to death. You are about to lose all your fight and die to your own will. That is your escape—dying to your self-will.

Deliverance comes not through resignation, but through resurrection. When Israel reached the Red Sea, with Pharaoh's army bearing down upon them, how did God deliver them? By doing away with the trouble? No, they weren't delivered until they went down into the Red Sea. This was a type of dying to the world— dying, that is, to trusting in their own flesh.

It is no great testimony to be able to say, "God gave me special faith. I spoke the Word, and all my troubles and sufferings and sicknesses ended. Praise God, I am free of all pain and affliction!" The much greater testimony is to be able to say, "No matter what lies ahead, no matter what the trial or affliction, God has proven

Himself faithful. He has produced in me life out of death. None of these afflictions can move me now. And now I can say with full confidence in His love, 'I consider that the sufferings of this present time are not worthy to be compared with the glory that shall be revealed in us.' "

And then, even in the midst of our pain, we will be able to offer true comfort to others—a sacrificial comfort that brings delight to the heart of Christ.

~ 15 ~
HE IS GOD OF OUR MONSTERS

We could not talk about suffering and trials, or even the subject of true versus false comfort, without looking at the life of the most troubled, distressed, despairing believer of all time. He was a righteous, God-loving man—yet when sorrow and trouble overwhelmed him, he sounded like an atheist. At the height of his suffering he concluded: "[Even] if I called and He answered me, I would not believe that He was listening to my voice. For He crushes me with a tempest, and multiplies my wounds without cause."

You have probably guessed that I am talking about Job. He is the man who lost everything—his family, wealth, goodwill, health and hope. The above quote is from chapter nine of the book bearing his name, and it is only one of the many despairing remarks that came from his lips as pain multiplied upon him.

All of Job's calamities came suddenly ("God doesn't even give me time to breathe between my bitter trials," see 9:18), and in his deepest despair he uttered these hopeless words: "[God] will laugh at the trial of the innocent" (9:23).

In so many words Job was saying, "It doesn't pay to be holy or walk uprightly. God treats the wicked and the pure the same way: They both suffer. So why labor to be upright?

"I was a praying man, loving God with all my heart. I was repentant, raising my children in the fear of the Lord. I was just and honest. I was kind and compassionate, caring for the poor and clothing the naked. And look what's happened to me. My life is all sorrow, trouble, hardship. No one really cares about me; no one is able to advise me. I don't have an intercessor. Oh, let God take His rod off my back; let Him stop terrifying me! All this is overwhelming! If God is at work in it, I certainly don't see it. In fact, my life is a joke, and God is mocking me in my sorrows."

The example of Job should be a great comfort to many of us because I believe he represents the last-day believer who will undergo great trials. I believe that in the days just ahead, multitudes of God-fearing, holy believers will go into the same fire that Job did. I don't know if we have already entered that time; but I do know we are swiftly nearing a time of trouble beyond all comprehension, a time the likes of which the world has never seen.

Already many wonderful, righteous Christians have lost their jobs or been out of work for weeks or months. Some have, like Job, been stripped bare, and many say they have never faced such hardship. Marriages are being tested, families are experiencing great heartache. Trouble is piling upon trouble. We have lost our young ones to the insanity of the hour. Our national and personal wealth is vanishing. Our health is declining as new diseases afflict people both young and old. As we look around, we find ourselves on the ash heap of despair.

And looking into the future can be a scary prospect because all we may be able to see is more uncertainty, fear and crisis. Our hearts may cry out, "What are we going to do? Why is all this happening to those of us who have been faithful to God? Why doesn't God intervene and stop it all?"

Consider this thought: What is happening to our generation is what happened to Job. There is much we can learn from his story.

The Accuser

I would be lying if I said that in the days ahead Christians will see trouble on all sides but will remain safe within a cozy cocoon of health and wealth. That will not happen. But just as God brought Job out of his affliction, He will bring us out as well.

I hear this message being preached from pulpits all across the nation. It is being proclaimed by many whom God has raised up as true prophetic voices, and they are preparing His people for what is ahead. Hundreds of ministers are gathering to pray in different cities, and they're hearing the same confession: "Never have so many been tested so deeply. In the past months something has been unleashed in the land. A flood of trouble, hardship, deep sorrow and suffering has befallen the godly."

That flood has an identity: Satan. He was Job's troubler, and he is our troubler right now. Is it possible he again is standing before God and issuing great accusations against the last-day Church? Might he be challenging God, "It is the last hour, true, but You have no true Church. You have no spotless Bride. They are not wise virgins. In fact, most of them are asleep! Look at them—they're materialistic, self-centered, grasping for riches and the good life. Listen to their teachers telling them they need not suffer, that all things are theirs for the asking. Take down Your wall of protection, God, and let me put them to the test. You won't have a holy remnant left! I'll smite them with sorrows, flood them with temptations and pour out on them a spirit of fear and despondency. I'll bring them to poverty. You'll see this pampered generation fold. They'll crumble and quit. There are no Jobs in this church—they're all spiritual wimps!"

This kind of scene is why Scripture says, "Woe to the inhabitants of the earth and the sea! For the devil has come down to you, having great wrath, because he knows that he has a short time" (Revelation 12:12).

Like Job we may cry out in confusion. We just don't realize how important it is to God that we trust Him through all the floods that come upon us. We know the devil cannot touch us unless God first lets down the wall and allows it—and I believe that wall is coming down now for all of us. Scripture is crystal clear in warning that in these last days God will put us through a purifying fire.

This is not, of course, the counsel Job heard. While Job was in his deepest despair, he was swamped by critics posing as counselors. They discouraged him further by pushing him to renounce the hidden sin in his life. God later told Job that all of their words were foolishness.

I have a warning for those who aren't suffering but who know a dear brother or sister who is. Maybe you have a Christian friend who's unemployed with no job in sight, or sudden calamity has struck his home, or problem after problem has popped up out of nowhere. When you see such a person discouraged by a trial, don't judge him. Only God can know his heart and whether or not sin lodges there. Instead put your arms around him and tell him, "I care for you." Weep with him who weeps, grieve with him who grieves. That's true counsel, because it comes straight from the Word of God.

It is a wicked thing to misrepresent God to those who are suffering. Don't add to your brother's sorrows; lift his burden, bear with him, weep with him, share his grief. Pray that God will give you His heart of compassion and sympathy, because you might be the next one to encounter the heat of affliction.

If you are suffering and the reason is not because God is dealing with sin in your life, then you will recognize true counsel that comes from praying people who are ordained of God and have the compassion of Jesus Christ. These ministers of comfort will come to you with the encouraging, edifying Word of God, and it will confirm what He has already spoken to you. You'll rejoice and say, "Thank God! Yes, that confirms what is in my heart. You've encouraged me that God has heard me!"

The Revelation

Our present suffering will end up producing one of two things in us: either hard-heartedness and a spirit of unbelief, or a glorious vision of God's control over everything concerning us. As for Job, he discovered in the midst of his suffering that despite all his knowledge of God, he didn't really know the Lord. He confessed, "I have heard of You by the hearing of the ear, but now my eye sees You. Therefore I abhor myself, and repent in dust and ashes" (Job 42:5–6).

Job was at least seventy years old at this time and he had been hearing about God all his life. He had spent many reverent hours praising God and worshiping at an altar erected to Him. His counselor friends had preached to him of the depths and mysteries of God. They had taught him about the consolations of God, the holiness of God, the character and nature of God and the wrath of God. They had spoken of the majesty of His power, His wisdom, His terror. But in a mind-boggling crisis, Job did not see God at all! God had become a vague theological term, a series of sermons, a dead word, a knowledge that had no life or power. Job had heard of God with his ears, but he had not seen God with the eye of his heart.

This is what God had to bring to the surface in Job. You see, He wants more than a holy man or woman kneeling at an altar, prostrate before Him, singing and extolling His praises. God wants a believer who can see Him in all he goes through; not as a God of the dead letter of the book, but as One who is all-knowing and ever near, One who has everything under control.

Sadly, many Christians today have built their house of faith on the sands of ease and goodness. When the storms of trial come, they will be blown away. Already I see Christians being blown apart in these last days. They don't understand the testings and trials of the Lord. They believe that because they've sought after God with all their heart, loved Him and longed after Him, they should be entitled to prosperity and a painless existence. They think every prayer should be answered immediately, with no trials at all.

But, as we have seen, the Bible doesn't say that the Lord will keep us from afflictions; it says He will *deliver us out of them.* And that's what God did for Job. In the middle of a whirlwind (representing trial and affliction), God appeared to Job to show him how to rise above his troubles. And He did this by making Job look into the face of two awesome monsters—the mighty hippopotamus and the serpent-like crocodile: "Look now at the behemoth [hippopotamus]" (Job 40:15). "Can you draw out Leviathan [crocodile] with a hook?" (41:1).

Why would God begin His revelation by having Job consider these two massive monsters?

First, He poses this problem to Job: "Here comes the hippopotamus. What are you going to do, wrestle him down? Sweet-talk him? And behold the crocodile. Can you put a rope in his nose? Play with him, tame him like a pet, bind him in your own power? Are you going to pry open his jaws and expose his teeth? He has a heart of stone, he has no mercy. He is king over all the children of pride."

This was more than a lecture about the strength and ferociousness of two awesome creatures. God was telling Job something about life's "monsters"—that the hippo and crocodile represented the monstrous problems raging in Job's life. He was saying, "If you try to fight these two creatures, you'll never forget the battle!"

The hippo tramples down everything in sight. He is a problem too big to handle. How do you wrestle down a hippo? Do you lasso him or bribe him with a bushel of corn? No, you are no match for him. Only the Lord knows how to stop a hippo.

The crocodile represents the demonic teeth that the devil flashes at you. No person can strip him of his armor using mere human strength. Only God can win a battle with him.

God was saying to Job and to all who will hear Him today, *Face the truth about the monsters in your life. You can't handle them. I'm the only One who can.*

I can imagine a little light suddenly clicking on in Job's head: "These monsters He's talking about—huge, overwhelming, fearless—they're my troubles. And I'll never wrestle them down! I've been sitting on this ash heap trying to figure out why God has permitted these monstrous problems to attack me, how I can fight them and chase them away. But I've forgotten that my God can do everything." Now Job's words were of a different tenor. He "answered the Lord, and said, 'I know that Thou canst do all things, and that no purpose of Thine can be thwarted' " (Job 42:1–2, NASB).

Suddenly Job saw clearly: "God is all-powerful. My life is not out of order. God *does* have a plan behind all my suffering. He is standing over me, sword in hand, to deliver me at the moment He sees fit. No man or monster can change His mind or affect His plan. My God will have His way. I can't stand up against the hippo or the crocodile—but I can stand still and see the salvation of the Lord!"

I learned this lesson years ago while working with Teen Challenge when, after walking the streets of New York City—worn out, broken in soul and body—I got mononucleosis. I ended up in the hospital for six weeks and developed a growth in my throat. I couldn't drink or swallow, and sometimes I couldn't even catch my breath. My weight soon fell under 115 pounds. I couldn't travel, and before long all our ministry's money dried up. It looked like the end of Teen Challenge. The crocodile was baring his teeth! So I lay flat on my back in the hospital, more than a little irritated at God. People came in to visit me, but they only made me nervous. And more than three counselors came in to give me "a word from the Lord" that only depressed me.

But I remember the night I said in desperation, "Lord, I give up, I can't fight it. It's all Yours—I'm just going to trust You. I have to ask just one thing of You. If you want the doors of Teen Challenge to close, that's Your business. But please, God, get this thing out of my throat!" Within an hour I coughed up a growth the size of a large walnut—and in that amount of time, I was well again. I left the hospital soon afterward and my strength started coming back. Most important, I discovered that while I was gone Teen Challenge had survived. I don't know how the Lord did it; it certainly wasn't through a miraculous big check! But while I was ill, the staff began to trust the Lord instead of looking to me. And that is what God was trying to accomplish all along.

Our troubles are not unforeseen accidents. And whatever we are going through, however deep the hurt, God is right on target and right on time in fighting our monsters. We may tend to think that the devil came in and interrupted God's plan, but that's not the case. If we are listening to His leading, hungering for close fellowship, ridding our lives of all that displeases Him, then He will harness everything meant for evil and turn it around for good.

Don't look back. Don't focus on your past mistakes. Get your eyes off the monsters! And don't let bitterness or self-pity destroy you. Encourage yourself with these words: "My God can do anything. He has not forgotten me. No one can change His plans. No matter how bad things look, God has everything under control."

You may ask, "Am I ever going to get out of this fiery trial? Will there be a happy ending, or will my suffering continue until Jesus comes? Will I ever rejoice again?"

Here is God's answer to you:

"You have heard of the perseverance of Job and seen the end intended by the Lord—that the Lord is very compassionate and merciful" (James 5:11). "The Lord restored Job's losses when he prayed for his friends. Indeed the Lord gave Job twice as much as he had before" (Job 42:10).

You may never double what you had, monetarily or otherwise, but you will possess something much greater: You will have a true heart-knowledge that God is in control of your life. You'll never again fear any adversary or hardship, because you will have come through seated in high places with Christ Jesus, more than a conqueror. Like Job, you may know God by hearing of Him, and that's good. That's where faith comes from. But now God wants you to *see* Him—to receive an absolute trust that He has a plan for your life, and that His eternal purpose cannot be thwarted by any demon in hell or any monster that appears in your path.

Then in the midst of the greatest trials of your life you can quote confidently one more verse from Job: "Though He slay me, yet will I trust Him" (13:15).

SECTION 3

GOD MEETS US IN OUR HUNGER

~ 16 ~
GOD WILL RESTORE OUR WASTED YEARS

"I will restore to you the years that the locust hath eaten, the canker-worm, and the caterpillar, and the palmerworm, my great army which I sent among you."

Joel 2:25, KJV

Hungering for more of Jesus, while opening us to trials, opens us to great blessings from His hand as well. As we draw closer to Him, we will hear His voice more clearly, warning, directing, wooing us, and we will find joy we have never known before.

But now we might wonder about all the time that it has taken us to get to this point. How many years did we waste before repenting and surrendering all to Jesus? How much of the past was eaten up by the cankerworm of sin and rebellion? We know we are forgiven and the past forgotten because it is all covered under the blood of Christ. But wouldn't it be wonderful to recapture those lost years and live them for the glory of the Lord?

In his final days the apostle Paul reflected on his life and testified, "I have fought a good fight, I have kept the faith. Now a crown of righteousness is awaiting me." As I read this passage not long ago, Paul's testimony pierced my soul. Something I couldn't shake nagged at my heart for weeks.

Finally in prayer I had to confess, "Lord, I don't think I can say that with Paul. I don't think I've fought a good fight of faith!" Perhaps I might be able to say that about the first fifteen years of my ministry and the last ten years, but there is a gap in that middle period during which I feel I wasted time. It was not that I resorted to some deep, dark sin, but rather that I drifted simply because I was not at my best for Jesus.

In my marriage, too, I look back with some shame because I wasted so many precious hours not nurturing and enjoying the relationship I have had with Gwen. I have been happily married to her for almost forty years now, and we are more in love than when we first married. Yet in recent years I have had to ask Gwen to forgive me for the times in midlife that I was arrogant and unkind, not at all the gentle, loving man God wanted me to be.

Perhaps, like me, you can look back with regret at wasted years. I think of a businessman in our church who threw away years by drinking and abusing drugs. He was an adulterer who left his wife for weeks at a time, a wild man driven by lust and greed. Today he is on fire for God, growing in Christ and wanting to make it all up to his wife. Yet he still feels the shame of those years that the cankerworm destroyed.

In fact, the closer you get to the heart of Jesus, the more those wasted years grieve you. The more you hunger for Christ, the more you cry out to Him from within: "Dear Lord, how could I have hurt You so? How could I have been so deceived? I took years that belonged to You and threw them away! O God, Your Word is so precious to me now, and I am so thrilled to be growing in the knowledge of You. How much growth in Christ I squandered, how much revelation I lost! How much blessing and anointing I forfeited!"

Yet here is an amazing thing: It doesn't matter if you have been walking with Christ for thirty years or thirty days; God can and will restore *all* your wasted years! The prophecy of Joel I quoted at the beginning of this chapter was directed to the nation of Israel, but it also applies to Christ's Body and to individual believers today. God has much to say to us in this prophecy—about both His character and our future.

Life Before Repentance

The entire second chapter of Joel speaks of a great army and the one directing it. Because Joel identifies the commander as God —"The Lord gives voice before His army" (Joel 2:11)—many interpret this passage to mean that huge numbers of godly soldiers are going forth to fight the Lord's battle against the enemy.

Not in this instance. This army is composed of spirits of destruction that Joel compares to locusts, palmerworms, caterpillars and cankerworms—all devouring insects. This great, dark army is employed by the Lord as a rod to execute His Word, for He calls it forth to bring down the wrath of His judgment. Joel said of this demonic army, "Sound the alarm in Zion! Warn them! Warn God's people that this army is coming to bring darkness and destruction!" (see Joel 2:1).

Joel gives us a picture here of an unrepentant people whom the enemy is given permission to attack. Thus the evil spirits rage like flames and burn everything in sight. These locusts are agents of war, climbing over every human wall of resistance, entering through every window of the mind and heart. Nothing can destroy them. The people are without defense and can only cringe, their faces full of sorrow.

Anyone who has been bound by a satanic habit knows what this is like. Your home—once a garden of life, full of peace and love— was soon devoured and left a desert wasteland. You tried to stop the attack but, like powerful horsemen, the destructive spirits leaped on you and were too strong for you to resist. One satanic worm after another devoured your life: "That which the palmerworm hath left hath the locust eaten; and that which the locust hath left hath the cankerworm eaten; and that which the cankerworm hath left hath the caterpillar eaten" (Joel 1:4, KJV).

Every vile movie, coke bag, bottle of wine, lurid novel, lustful thought becomes a locust, a cankerworm. Doesn't that describe what happens to every unrepentant soul? Satan has his teeth clamped on him or her, and his "teeth are the teeth of a lion" (Joel 1:6). He causes waste, ruin and mourning. Everything is devoured. "The vine has dried up, and the fig tree has withered . . . all the trees of the field are withered . . . joy has withered away" (verse 12).

Think back to your own life before your salvation. Do you recall this same terrible destruction? You were dying both physically and spiritually; you were totally helpless to fight the hordes of hell. And then you met Jesus.

Full Restoration

"I will restore to you the years that the locust hath eaten" (Joel 2:25, KJV). The New American Standard Bible says, "I will make up to you for the years . . . eaten." What an incredible promise!

After seeing how I had failed the Lord, I wanted to make up those years to God, to make amends and repay Him. But He said, *No, you can't repay Me for a single wasted hour. I will make it all up to you! All those years of being wasted, stripped and harassed by the devil will be restored to you. Walk before Me in righteousness and turn from your sins and I will make up all the losses, whether they were yours, your loved ones' or Mine.*

We need not be ashamed of our wasted years because when God removes the evil army from us we will eat and be satisfied. To all repentant sinners He declares, "Fear not! Be glad and rejoice for the Lord will do great things. You will never again be ashamed" (see Joel 2:19–21, 26–27).

Now, because of Christ, everything is new *including the calendar*! The Lord goes back to the day the locusts came in, removes all those wasted years and starts counting again from the moment we repented. All those blessings we missed have been stored up. All the joy, peace and usefulness that seemed dead and gone were actually kept by the Lord. In hell, the damned may be haunted with a vision of what their lives could have been. Jesus implies they may see what they lost (see Luke 16:19–31). But this is not so for the repentant because all will be restored to us. We need never again say, "Oh, what I missed, what I could have been! Oh, how much God had for me, but I blew it." God can restore all those wasted blessings!

In the Old Testament we read that God commanded a sabbath year in Israel to take place every seventh year. The Israelites were to allow the land to rest in that year and not be cultivated. But the people wondered what they would eat. So God told them: "And if you say, 'What shall we eat in the seventh year, since we shall not sow nor gather in our produce?' Then I will command My blessing on you in the sixth year, and it will bring forth produce enough for three years" (Leviticus 25:20–21). The Lord of the harvest had only to speak, and the need would be met abundantly.

The same is true for every believer today. God need only speak a word to restore any abundance. God restores our wasted years by producing in us supernatural joy, revelation, peace and victory far beyond our human comprehension. He can accomplish more in us, for us and through us now than we ever thought possible. We can stand upright today as if we had never sinned, as if we had lost no time, as if we were right where we would have been had the devourer never come. God puts us right back on His divine schedule. His eternal purpose and plan are exactly where He planned them to be: Nothing is lost to Him. And we need dwell on it no longer.

Pressing On

Paul states it this way: "Forgetting those things which are behind and reaching forward to those things which are ahead, I press toward the goal for the prize of the upward call of God in Christ Jesus" (Philippians 3:13–14). In other words, Paul is instructing us, "Forget your past and press on in Jesus!"

This instruction is vital because Satan's favorite harassment is to scare you by bringing old skeletons from your past out of the closet. He will try to persuade you that an old habit, addiction or lust will rise up again and bring back the devourer. You can react to this in one of three ways: You can fall back into the old temptation. Or you can begin to think you cannot fall, and thus succumb to pride (and then you will have already fallen!). Or, finally, you can do what is right—and if you do, who can possibly harm you? You might feel the pangs of remorse for your waste as long as you live. And, yes, the memories will keep you humble. But in God's eyes, your past is a dead issue. As far as condemnation and guilt are concerned, God says, "Forget the past—I've taken care of that. Press on to what I have promised you!"

Are you being devoured even now? Are the worms of the devil eating away at your life? If so, you can start all over again, right now. In fact, God's law of restoration can begin making everything new this very hour. Your past can be wiped clean, and this can be the first day of a new life for you in Christ. The Bible gives us a picture of such restoration in the New Testament, when Jesus healed a man with a withered hand: "He said to the man, 'Stretch out your hand.' And he stretched it out, and it was restored as whole as the other" (Matthew 12:13).

Be encouraged that as we are restored in Jesus our old wounds can't even be found. So take any worries and heart-naggings about wasted years to God today, and let Him begin His restoring work. Press onward, straight ahead, toward the prize of your high calling in Him, then watch in wonder as the blessings that were taken away are restored to you in overflowing abundance.

17

THE GOD OF HOPE

Some time ago, a distraught woman wrote to me:

I am terrified! I think it would be wonderful if hydrogen bombs fell on us, especially on me and my family. Then it would all be over for us in a hurry, and we'd be with Jesus! I am a retired widow with no man in our family. I lost my husband to cancer. I just got out of the hospital and am recovering from a broken back. I have two unmarried daughters, one who has health problems and hasn't worked in two years. We have suffered terribly for the past sixteen years. Members of our fellowship are being persecuted, and my friends are all suffering unmercifully. Fear and anxiety are my lot in life. Mr. Wilkerson, we are hurting! Is there no hope for the Bride of Christ? Please answer!

This woman is just one of thousands who write our ministry of their despair and hopelessness. We hear from many who love the Lord deeply but who live in situations and conditions that appear hopeless to them. They speak of dead-end marriages, family conflicts and health problems. They use these phrases:

"There's no way out!"

"I brought it on myself. Now I'm in a prison, stuck for life."

"God doesn't seem to hear me, because nothing ever changes. And if it does, things only go from bad to worse."

"Sometimes I wonder if it's worth it. I wish the Lord would come pull me out of this pit."

"I have a few good days. But then this feeling overwhelms me that I'm worthless, just doing nothing."

It has been said that the only thing worse than insanity is despair. But, praise the Lord, we serve a God who will fill us with hope! The Greek word for *hope* is *elpo*, meaning "to look forward to with pleasurable confidence and expectation." The apostle Paul wrote to the Romans, "Now may the God of hope fill you with all joy and peace in believing, that you may abound in hope by the power of the Holy Spirit" (Romans 15:13).

Paul introduces an incredible idea in this passage—that we "may *abound in hope*." He means that we "may have enough to spare, a supply that is overflowing, excessive, beyond measure." Some of you may think, "That sounds like a cruel joke. In my present condition all I want is a ray of hope—just one small evidence of answered prayer!" But this passage in God's Word is as true as every other. He *is* a God of hope—a hope that is excessive, over-flowing and beyond measure. And Paul's prayer for all believers is that He "fill you with all joy and peace in believing." This is to be the normal state for all Christians—not just for well-adjusted, happy-go-lucky believers, but for all! God does not mock His hurt-ing children today. No, He truly is *now* a God of hope, ready to flood our souls with exceeding, overflowing joy and peace.

Paul stated,

For we were saved in this hope, but hope that is seen is not hope; for why does one still hope for what he sees? But if we hope for what we do not see, we eagerly wait for it with perseverance.

Romans 8:24–25

Our response, however, is usually a demand to see change: "I would have hope if I could just see a small bit of evidence that God is working for my good—just a little something to get hold of. I need to see something change. How can I have hope when months go by and things only get worse?" But to abound in hope is to have excessive, overflowing perseverance and patience—more than enough to wait for God's answers. Joy and peace come only when you know God has everything under control.

Misplaced Trust

Hopelessness is the result of trusting in man:

Thus says the Lord: "*Cursed* is the man who trusts in man and makes flesh his strength, whose heart departs from the Lord. For he shall be like a shrub in the desert, and shall not see when good comes, but shall inhabit the parched places in the wilderness, in a salt land which is not inhabited. *Blessed* is the man who trusts in the Lord, and whose hope is the Lord. For he shall be like a tree planted by the waters, which spreads out its roots by the river, and will not fear when heat comes; but its leaf will be green, and will not be anxious in the year of drought, nor will cease from yielding fruit."

Jeremiah 17:5–8, emphasis mine

Jeremiah introduces here two immutable laws of spiritual life. One leads to death and hopelessness, the other to life and hope. These laws are the keys to understanding why some Christians enjoy constant peace and joy in the Lord while others grope in despair.

The Hebrew word Jeremiah uses for *cursed* means "utterly detestable." In other words, the person who departs from God and leans instead on man is utterly detestable to Him. How can we know when we are trusting in man rather than in God? If we come apart when someone lets us down, or if the actions of others affect our walk with God, then we know our trust is in man—that is, in something or someone other than God. Christians who put their trust in man in order to provide safety for themselves are guaranteed to get hurt. At some point, someone is going to let them down and disappoint them deeply. "The heart is deceitful above all things, and desperately wicked; who can know it?" (Jeremiah 17:9). Just when they think they know someone, they're in for a shock. They end up saying, "I never expected that of him."

A woman may argue, for instance, "My husband really has hurt me. He neglects me all the time, and he doesn't even try to understand. His words cut me so deeply; he is killing my love. If only he'd change, then I could be happy!"

No, I'm afraid that wife wouldn't be happy. When the Bible talks about putting "no confidence in the flesh" (Philippians 3:3), it means our *own* flesh. Even if that husband became a perfect mate, saying kind things and treating her like a queen, it would not change her. She would not see the good in it because *her heart* would not be changed. She would still despair; in fact, she would feel worse because her problem is not with her husband or anyone else. It is with her. It is a God-problem. She is trusting in someone other than Him to bring her happiness and hope.

Jeremiah describes this as being a shrub in the desert, not seeing the river but instead inhabiting the parched places in the wilderness. It is being cut off from the true supply of happiness and hope. By neglecting the Lord, this woman and those like her are not drawing on His living water. They have become like dry desert shrubs—fruitless and barren!

One of the great manmade wonders in America is the incredible New York aqueduct. It took a whole army of Italian immigrants to build it. It is made of bricks, is underground and runs for miles and miles from upstate bringing water to New York City. Now what would happen if this aqueduct were cut off, and suddenly there was no water supply flowing to the city? New York would become one of the "parched places . . . a salt land which is not inhabited."

This is what can happen in our lives. Many Christians today lose hope, turning inward instead of running to the Lord. But God is saying to His people, "You are in despair simply because you do not trust in Me. You turn to others—to doctors, medicine, friends, counselors, finances. You are not uplifted by My promises—yet you let the words of men cast you down. You have cursed yourself by not coming to Me. You are dry, empty and lonely because you do not draw water from My well."

Jeremiah describes further "the sin of Judah" (17:1). God's own people sinned in difficult times by not turning to Him in faith and instead seeking help from their own flesh:

> "The virgin of Israel has done a very horrible thing. Will a man leave the snow water of Lebanon, which comes from the rock of the field? Will the cold waters be forsaken for strange waters?"
>
> Jeremiah 18:13–14

Like the cold, refreshing waters that flow down from melting snow, God gives an unceasing supply of power to His people. In this passage, Lebanon's water is a steady stream of strength, always available and never failing. Yet God's people often continue on their way dry, empty and sad, saying, "We have been left to ourselves. We'll just go our own forsaken way, unwanted." This is a picture of despairing Christians who have forgotten the promises of God, who sit dejected beside a flowing stream of God's love, thinking, "The Lord is not at work in my life. I'm just going to have to grit my teeth and do the best I can. I'll fight alone if I have to. It's no use hoping anymore. I'll just have to do what I can to survive."

How God must continue to grieve over this today when He hears the language of hopelessness spoken by so many downcast Christians! I shudder when I hear believers use these words of despair: "It's no use. There's no hope!" It is the same language Israel used when they despaired: "And they said, There is no hope" (Jeremiah 18:12, KJV).

There is a great danger in remaining hopeless:

> "Because My people have forgotten Me, they have burned incense to worthless idols. And they have caused themselves to stumble . . . to walk in pathways and not on a highway."
>
> Jeremiah 18:15

Our city streets and bars are filled with despairing people. They are the walking wounded, throwing away their lives and perhaps still trying to get even with someone who hurt them. Some are people who got mad at God for not helping them in a certain way when they wanted Him to.

I know of one minister's wife who plunged into a deep depression. She was sick from all the gossip and trouble in their church and she thought God was not helping them with their problems. Finally she told her husband, "I can't take it anymore." She left him and their two children and ran off with an unsaved man. She now spends her time drinking in bars.

I could write a book about all the tragedies of people I know who have grown so depressed and hopeless that they have become reckless with their lives. If people allow the devil to convince them that they are helpless victims—worthless, good for nothing and for no one—he can make them do things they never thought possible (including suicide). This depression can also lead to spiritual laziness. People give themselves excuses to do nothing about their situations. "Just leave me alone," they say. "I'll figure it out on my own." They believe God has forgotten them. But Scripture says their problems have taken place "because [God's] people have forgotten [Him]."

Depression, dryness and hopelessness are the direct results of being cut off from our daily supply of living water. When we neglect faith, prayer and the Word—our access to the flowing snow-waters of Lebanon—the result is always loneliness, fruitlessness and emptiness.

The One Who Hopes

Thank God there is another immutable law—the law of hope and life! "He shall be like a tree planted by the rivers of water" (Psalm 1:3). This verse contains the secret of living in constant hope and is the lifeline of those hungering for Jesus. It's not found in trying to reform, in attempting to please people or in making promises to God we can't keep. The person who experiences this promise can no longer be hurt by people because he does not hope in them. His expectations instead are all in the Lord. He does not care what man says or does; his eyes are on the Lord alone. And the Lord never fails him or lets him down.

"He shall be like a tree planted by the rivers of water." An amazing Hebrew word is used here for *planted.* It actually means "transplanted." Faith uproots the scorched desert-shrub and transplants it by the living stream of the waters flowing from Lebanon. David said this about the Lord: "You visit the earth and water it, you greatly enrich it; the river of God is full of water. . . . You bless its growth" (Psalm 65:9–10).

This river of God heals everything it touches. If we put our roots down deep in His river, we will not fear when the heat comes. For our "leaf [appearance] shall be green [fresh, alive]." The dry spells will not affect us and we will bear fruit constantly. We will not be continually tired, weeping, lonely, dry and feeling forsaken. Instead, we will be refreshed and renewed simply by resting in His Word.

Why do some believers always rejoice and abound in hope? Why do they seem so full of peace and joy, radiating the glow of spiritual life and health? Is it because they don't have any problems? No—in fact, they probably have more problems than most people. But they have learned the secret of having roots in God's river.

If you are rooted in the river, you don't always need a revival. You don't need "showers of blessings," a special outpouring or a sudden flood of victory. If you enjoy an hour-by-hour flow of life-giving water, you're not constantly moving from dry spell to blessing, from lows to highs, from coldness to revival. Spiritual famine doesn't touch you, and the scorching heat of apostasy doesn't faze you, because you are drawing water from the steady flow of God's river of life. If I had to choose between revival and roots, I'd take roots any day. For long after revival is gone my roots would supply me daily with all I need.

The prophet Ezekiel was given a vision of the New Jerusalem and saw a stream pouring out of the Temple (see chapter 47). As he watched, the stream swelled from a trickle to a rushing flow. He then saw a man measuring this growing stream of life, until it became a river. On the banks of this river stood many trees, all green and bearing fruit:

"Along the bank of the river . . . will grow all kinds of trees used for food; their leaves will not wither, and their fruit will not fail. They will bear fruit every month, because their water flows from the sanctuary. Their fruit will be for food, and their leaves for medicine."

Ezekiel 47:12

What do these trees signify? They represent all those with roots of trust in the Lord.

"And it shall be that every living thing that moves, wherever the rivers go, will live. There will be a very great multitude of fish, because these waters go there; for they will be healed, and everything will live wherever the river goes."

Ezekiel 47:9

And this river is Jesus! His very presence refreshes and renews us. The moment we cast down all doubt and fear, crying out, "O Lord, in You I have abounding hope," we will be transplanted to the banks of this river by the power of the Holy Ghost. And it is important to get our roots down deep in God's hope now, because the worst is yet to come:

"If you have run with the footmen, and they have wearied you, then how can you contend with horses? And if in the land of peace . . . they wearied you, then how will you do in the floodplain of the Jordan?"

Jeremiah 12:5

A great time of distress is coming soon upon the earth, but as we hunger for Jesus, hoping in Him, we will be sending our roots down by the river, digging deep into the secret reservoir of His life. And doing this is the only way to cheer our hearts and remain glad.

To those who wait patiently and expectantly on God, "the Lord will command His lovingkindness in the daytime, and in the night His song shall be with [us]" (Psalm 42:8). Christ will turn our hopelessness into rejoicing and clothe us with gladness—if we put our faith and trust in Him. "You have turned for me my mourning into dancing; You have put off my sackcloth and clothed me with gladness" (Psalm 30:11).

Because He has everything under control, because we are rooted in the river of His abundance, we can abound in hope.

Let us rejoice in the God of hope—and *live!*

~ 18 ~

THE LOVINGKINDNESS OF THE LORD

I know that if we hunger for God He will pour out His loving-kindness on us, but this is one aspect of the Lord's character that I know very little about. I believe few Christians do. During my lifetime, I have experienced and preached much about God's righteous judgments, His holy fear, His justice and holiness, His hatred for sin. But I haven't understood or preached much about His lovingkindness.

While in prayer, the Holy Spirit spoke clearly to my heart about this subject. He said, *David, the road is indeed straight and the gate is narrow that leads to salvation. But don't try to make My way straighter and narrower than My Word makes it!*

Needless to say, that hit me. I reached for my concordance and very soon I discovered how much the Bible says about the loving-kindness of the Lord. Again and again we can read these wonderful words spoken by Moses, the prophets, the apostles: "Your God is merciful, kind, gracious, anxious to forgive, full of lovingkindness, slow to anger" (see Exodus 34:6; Deuteronomy 4:31; Joel 2:13; Jonah 4:2; Romans 2:4). I must confess, I have never truly pictured the Lord this way. Such knowledge of Him is in my head—it always has been—but I have never truly experienced it in my heart.

Moses thundered prophetic warnings to Israel about impending judgment, but Moses also had a great revelation of the Lord's lovingkindness. In the cloud of God's presence, the Lord revealed to Moses His nature:

> Now the Lord descended in the cloud and stood with him there, and proclaimed the name of the Lord. And the Lord passed before him and proclaimed, "The Lord, the Lord God, merciful and gracious, longsuffering, and abounding in goodness and truth, keeping mercy for thousands, forgiving iniquity and transgression and sin."
>
> Exodus 34:5–7

In spite of all the warnings of judgment that Moses preached, he always remembered God's mercy. He said, "When you turn to the Lord your God and obey His voice (for the Lord your God is a merciful God), He will not forsake you nor destroy you" (Deuteronomy 4:30–31).

In the Old Testament, God's people forsook Him time after time. Yet each time He restored them and gave them incredible blessings. The Lord had every right to give up on Israel, but instead He remained faithful to them. Nehemiah sums up this wonderful revelation:

> "But after they had rest, they again did evil before You. . . . Yet when they returned and cried out to You, You heard from heaven; and many times You delivered them according to Your mercies. . . . In Your great mercy You did not utterly consume them nor forsake them; for You are God, gracious and merciful."
>
> Nehemiah 9:28, 31

Isaiah also preached often about God's vengeance against sin. He told of dark days of doom and despair coming upon those who live in rebellion against God. Yet in the middle of one of his most frightening messages about the Lord's day of wrath, Isaiah stopped and cried out,

I will mention the lovingkindnesses of the Lord and the praises of the Lord, according to all that the Lord has bestowed on us . . . according to His mercies, according to the multitude of His lovingkindnesses.

Isaiah 63:7

In the midst of all the sin, apostasy and rebellion in Israel, Isaiah could look deep into his own heart and recall a revelation of what God was truly like. He cried, "O Lord, we have rebelled against You and vexed Your Holy Spirit. But save us again by Your pity. Stir up Your mercy toward us, for You are full of lovingkindness."

The prophet Joel also warned of the coming days of darkness, full of devouring flames, massive earthquakes and the darkening of the sun and moon. But then, like Isaiah, the prophet stopped and, in the midst of dire warnings about wrath and judgment, prophesied:

"Now, therefore," says the Lord, "turn to Me with all your heart, with fasting, with weeping, and with mourning." So rend your heart, and not your garments; return to the Lord your God, for He is gracious and merciful, slow to anger, and of great kindness; and He relents from doing harm.

Joel 2:12–13

He relents means that God wants to change His mind about the judgment He has planned. He doesn't *want* to judge; instead, He hopes we will mourn over our sins and turn to Him for forgiveness.

As I said, for years I, too, have prophesied judgment concerning the Body of Christ. And I will continue to prophesy until Jesus comes, if He will allow me. But lately I have sensed the Lord saying to me, *No prophet in My Book could prophesy until he first had a revelation of My lovingkindness. You, too, must first understand this aspect of My character.*

Understanding His Lovingkindness

Thus says the Lord: "Let not the wise man glory in his wisdom, let not the mighty man glory in his might, nor let the rich man glory in his riches; but let him who glories glory in this, that he understands and knows Me, that I am the Lord, exercising lovingkindness, judgment, and righteousness in the earth. For in these I delight," says the Lord.

Jeremiah 9:23–24

I have never had any trouble confessing my sin. To the best of my knowledge, I have not tried to excuse or hide my failings, and I have always run to the Lord right away when He has revealed sin in my life. Yet still, whenever I fail the Lord and know that I have grieved Him, I become overwhelmed with shame, guilt, condemnation and unworthiness. I preach to others that the Lord is gracious and forgiving. But when *I* fail God, it suddenly becomes a different matter.

You ask, "Aren't we supposed to experience those feelings when we sin?" Of course we are. But we are not supposed to continue for days and weeks thinking God is mad at us. The guilt and condemnation should lift quickly. You see, even after I repent, I feel I have to make it all up to the Lord. Like the Prodigal Son, I can have the Father hugging my neck, kissing my cheek, putting rings on my fingers and a robe on my back; He can tell me to forget the past, to come inside His house and enjoy the feast He has prepared for me. But I say, "I can't go in—I'm not worthy! I've sinned against You. Let me pay You back. Let me grieve and carry the guilt a little longer." It is easy for me to believe that God forgave Israel, Nineveh, the heathen, the dying thief. But I find it hard to understand how, the very moment I turn to Him with all *my* heart, He quickly and lovingly accepts me as if I had not sinned.

"Whoever is wise will observe these things, and they will understand the lovingkindness of the Lord" (Psalm 107:43). David received the awesome revelation of God's gracious, forgiving heart simply by looking at His record of dealing with His beloved children. David relates the key to understanding God's lovingkindness in this particular psalm. And that key is simple and uncomplicated: *'Then they cried out to the Lord. . . ."* It is repeated four times in Psalm 107.

The children of Israel wandered away from the Lord in the wilderness, hungry and thirsty, lost because of sin. *"Then they cried out to the Lord in their trouble, and He delivered them out of their distresses"* (verse 6). Yet again they rebelled and backslid. They fell so low they were at the very gates of hell. *"Then they cried out to the Lord in their trouble. . . . He brought them out of darkness and the shadow of death and broke their chains in pieces"* (verses 13–14). Once more they found themselves suffering greatly, afflicted and unable to eat because of their transgressions. *'Then they cried out to the Lord in their trouble. . . . He sent His word and healed them"* (verses 19–20). Whenever God's people come to their wits' end, when storms are raging and trouble melts their souls, *"Then they cry out to the Lord in their trouble, and He brings them out of their distresses. He calms the storm, so that its waves are still"* (verses 28–29).

Here is what the Lord was teaching David: "Simply look at My record. Observe all My dealings with the children of Israel. They failed Me and failed Me. But when they cried out to Me, I heard them. My nature is touched by the tears of my children and moved with compassion when they return to Me. I am touched by the feeling of their infirmities."

In response to this revelation, David is saying in this psalm, "Look how easily God's heart is moved, how quickly He responds to the cries of His children. There is no end to His mercies!" We don't have to continue experiencing agony and guilt; we don't have to run to a counselor or call a friend. We can simply go to the Lord and cry out in confession to Him. He is a tender Father who is touched by our needs.

I think David appreciated this revelation from the Lord all the more because of his own experiences of sinning. Because his heart was so tender toward the Lord, he must have been miserable after committing adultery and murder. I believe David wept in sorrow the very night he fell into adultery. Such a Spirit-filled man of God could not operate day after day without carrying an agonizing burden of shame, guilt and fear.

I recall the times I have been in a room when pastors or church members who truly love God have been confronted with their sin. Those who are close to the Lord have nearly always broken down crying, "Yes, yes, it's true! How could I have done it? My sin has been ever before me. O God, forgive me—I want help!" This undoubtedly happened when Nathan confronted David. Through the prophet, God told the king of Israel, "You have brought reproach upon My name." Then, while David was still weeping, Nathan assured him, "Your sins are forgiven."

But those words were not enough for David. It is one thing to be forgiven, and quite another to be free and clear with the Lord. David knew that forgiveness was the easy part. Now he wanted to get things right with God, to be able to have his joy back. So after this episode he cried, "Do not cast me away from Your presence, and do not take Your Holy Spirit from me" (Psalm 51:11). Then throughout Psalm 51 David remembers the longsuffering and mercy of the Lord.

Like David, we, too, must find victory over sin by having absolute confidence in this one thing: No matter how grievously we have sinned or fallen, *we serve a Lord who is ready to forgive, anxious to heal and who possesses more lovingkindness toward us than we could ever need.* The devil will come to us and say, "No! If you get off the hook too easily, you'll jump right back into sin." He will try to make us feel miserable, dirty, unworthy to lift our hands in praise to God or even to pick up His Word. But here is our weapon: *Cry!* We must cry out as David did, *with all our hearts!* Cry out as the Israelites did, throwing ourselves totally upon the mercy of the Lord. We can go to God, confess our sin, appeal to His lovingkindness. We can say, "Lord, I know You love me, and Your Word says You're ready to forgive me. O Lord, I confess!"

At that very moment, we are clear with God. We do not have to pay for our sin. God loves us so much that He gave His Son, Jesus, *who has already paid for it.* A merciful, loving Advocate is yearning to help and deliver us: "My little children, these things I write to you, so that you may not sin. And if anyone sins, we have an Advocate with the Father, Jesus Christ the righteous" (1 John 2:1).

Not long ago I was strolling with my young granddaughter and she wanted to walk atop a low wall. I held her from behind to keep her from falling, but she tried to push my hand away. Eventually I let go and she toppled over without hurting herself. Yet when she fell, I didn't desert her. I didn't say, "Look at what you did. You're not mine anymore!"

The Lord spoke to me through this: *You allow yourself such love for this child. But you won't allow Me to love you in the same way. You swell with pride over your children, but you won't allow Me to do so with you.* Not long after that, the Lord spoke yet another tender word to my heart. He said, *David, you bless Me. You bless My heart!* No one has ever said anything better to me in my life. What joy in knowing that, as the Bible says, God takes pleasure in His children!

Enjoying His Lovingkindness

Jonah was a prophet who fully understood the lovingkindness of the Lord, yet he could not enjoy or appropriate it. Instead, it was a burden to him. When God commanded him to go to the wicked city Nineveh and prophesy its quick destruction, Jonah ran in the other direction. Later, he told the Lord why he had run away: It was because of His lovingkindness!

Here was Jonah's argument: "Lord, You've commanded me to walk up and down the streets of Nineveh, prophesying that they have only forty days before it's all over. But I can't do that because I know You. You are easily touched. Tears and repentance soften Your heart. I know what will happen: They'll repent and You'll change Your mind. Instead of sending judgment, You'll send a revival and I'll end up looking like a fool."

Jonah did eventually go to Nineveh, but only by way of the belly of a giant fish, who spat him up onto dry ground. Finally, the prophet proclaimed the judgment of God—and, sure enough, Nineveh did repent (even though the prophet's message mentioned nothing about repentance, only destruction). These sin-hardened, wicked Ninevites wept, fasted, mourned and put on sackcloth, even on their animals! It was one of the most sweeping revivals ever recorded in the Bible.

In the midst of all this, Jonah grew angry. He must have prayed: "I knew this would happen. You send me out on those streets crying, 'Judgment, bloodshed, fire!' Then they call on You, and as soon as You see the first tear fall You change your mind. I knew it because I know You. You are slow to anger, eager to forgive and ready to send peace and blessing instead of calamity."

I have to confess, I know how Jonah must have felt. Not long ago I had a little egg on my face, too. Our ministry warned America that God might judge us on the battlefield of Kuwait and Iraq, echoing Abraham Lincoln's belief that all war is a sign of God's judgment. We proclaimed that America had not repented nor had our leaders called for nationwide repentance, and we feared a great effusion of blood. During one of our church's Friday night prayer meetings, I said, "How can God be with our armies when we have so much blood on our hands? The Bible is full of accounts of God giving up on His armies when the people sinned as we have. We face judgment!"

Instead, victory came swiftly. After only one hundred hours of ground fighting, the war was over, one of the most lopsided conflicts in history. Soon I got a letter from someone who used to attend our church. It said, "You lied! There was no judgment. God was with our armies and there were no thousands dead. Your warning was not from God."

Here is what I believe happened: Once again, the Lord's gracious heart was easily moved. Hundreds of thousands of soldiers and believers around the world suddenly cried out to God, "Help us, give us one more chance!" Churches all over the world held prayer meetings, crying out, "O God, forgive us! Cleanse us from our sin!" One reporter in Saudi Arabia said, "Never have I heard so many soldiers praying or singing spiritual songs. Never have I seen so many reading the Bible. It was like church!"

I believe God was moved with compassion. He was moved and touched, because He is so ready to forgive. Like Jonah, I should have known He is "slow to anger and abundant in lovingkindness, One who relents from doing harm" (Jonah 4:2). Instead of pouring out judgment on America, God used our army as His rod against Saddam Hussein. God was with America! Our gracious Lord took pity on us and changed His mind as surely as He changed His mind about Nineveh. And I believe the tears and repentance of believers brought forth this great lovingkindness.

I pray the Church doesn't make the same mistake Jonah did and fail to enjoy God's lovingkindness. We need to thank Him for His great mercy toward us, that He heard the cry of our nation—and answered!

Joy and His Lovingkindness

The Bible says the joy of the Lord is our strength and without it we have no power to stand. We must be on our guard, because guilt and condemnation for sin absolutely destroy the joy of the Lord.

Now, those who still cling to sin and refuse to return to the Lord's fullness have no right to the joy of the Lord. In fact, the Bible says they will have a troubled countenance. When Judah sinned God said, "I will take from them the voice of mirth [laughter] and the voice of gladness" (Jeremiah 25:10). Included in the punishment for sin is the loss of all joy: "The joy of our heart has ceased; our dance has turned into mourning" (Lamentations 5:15). The Christian who has something to hide can't actually hide anything, because the change caused by sin is written all over his face. It is evident in his walk, talk and appearance. If you ask him, "How are you doing?" you will likely hear the answer, "Well, so-so. I'm just barely making it." He has no shout, no sign of victory—only a look of despair, sadness and dejection. There can be no joy or vibrancy where sin is lurking.

If in hungering for Jesus we have repented of sin we must not allow the devil to rob us of our right to rejoice and be glad. As we accept God's forgiveness then we can worship and praise Him joyfully. Throughout Scripture God pours out His oil of gladness on those who love His righteousness: "Be glad in the Lord and rejoice, you righteous; and shout for joy, all you upright in heart" (Psalm 32:11). "Let the righteous be glad; let them rejoice before God; yes, let them rejoice exceedingly" (Psalm 68:3). "Let all those who seek you rejoice and be glad in You" (Psalm 70:4). And the Word says of Jesus: "You have loved righteousness and hated lawlessness; therefore God, Your God, has anointed You with the oil of gladness more than Your companions" (Hebrews 1:9).

Some Christians picture Jesus only as weeping in the Garden, sweating great drops of blood. Yes, He did spend nights in agony, praying all alone. But I believe when He came down from those quiet times with God, He had laughter in His soul. He could clap His hands and dance and praise His heavenly Father!

People who have forsaken their sins and are walking with the Lord may still have an unresolved struggle. But there is such a drawing toward the Lord in them, such a hunger for Christ, that the outcome is inevitable: They experience an overwhelming outbreak of joy! True heart-confession and a desire for the Lord open up rivers of praise and a fountain of thanksgiving.

Perhaps the following scenario will help you picture the Lord's lovingkindness more clearly: Suppose Jesus appears in the flesh, dressed as an ordinary man, and sits next to you in church. You are a defeated Christian, sitting there wounded, wearing a look of gloom, guilt, condemnation and fear. You do not recognize Him and He begins to talk to you:

"Do you really love the Lord?" He asks.

You answer, "Very much so!"

"You've sinned, haven't you?"

"Y-yes," you say (hoping this isn't a prophet who can read your mind!).

"Do you believe He forgives any and all who confess and turn from their sins?"

"Yes, but . . . I've hurt my Savior. I've truly wounded Him."

"Why haven't you appropriated His forgiveness? If you've confessed, why haven't you received it?"

"I've done it so many times!"

"Do you believe He will forgive 490 times—if each time you confess and repent?"

"Yes."

"Even murder? adultery? homosexuality? drugs? jealousy? hatred?"

"Yes."

"Do you hate your sin? Do you still want Him?"

"Oh, yes!"

"Then why are you letting the devil rob you of the victory of the cross, the power of the blood of the Lamb? Why aren't you appropriating His joy?"

I hope that by picturing this scene we can all remember that we don't have to give up our joy in the Lord. We have a right to praise Him—to sing, shout and be happy in Him!

Proclaiming His Lovingkindness

Scripture says clearly that we are to preach about the Lord's lovingkindness to all mankind. David said,

> I have not hidden Your righteousness within my heart; I have declared Your faithfulness and Your salvation; I have not concealed Your lovingkindness and Your truth from the great assembly.
>
> Psalm 40:10

David did not just appropriate this wonderful message for himself. He knew it was also sorely needed by the whole congregation and by a hurting world. He was grateful to God for such great love because he was aware of his own failings. It doesn't matter how badly people have sinned—God still *loves*. That's why He sent His Son. And that is what we should be preaching to the world. Can we say with David, "I have not concealed Your lovingkindness from the great assembly"? That is His desire for all of us.

Perhaps one of the most quoted and sung verses in all of God's Word is this: "Because Your lovingkindness is better than life, my lips shall praise You" (Psalm 63:3). What does it mean, "His lovingkindness is better than life"? The fact is, life is short. It fades like the grass, which is here one season and gone the next. But God's lovingkindness will endure forever. A billion years from now, Jesus will be as tender and loving to us as He is this minute. People may take someone's life, but they can't take away God's eternal lovingkindness.

Stop and think about it for a moment: God is not mad at us anymore. The Word says that *nothing* can come between our Lord and us—no guilt, no torment, no condemning thoughts. We can say, "My life is a blessing to the Lord, and I can rejoice and praise Him. I am clean, free, forgiven, justified, sanctified and redeemed!"

We have a loving, tender Father who cares about us. And as we begin to understand how compassionate He is toward us—how patient, how caring, how ready to forgive and bless—we will not be able to contain ourselves. We will shout and praise until we have no voice left: "His lovingkindness truly is better than life!"

19

HE WILL HELP US BE FAITHFUL

The book of Hebrews offers this strong, vital word to all believers:

> Holy brethren, partakers of the heavenly calling, consider the Apostle and High Priest of our confession, Christ Jesus, who was faithful to Him who appointed Him, as Moses also was faithful in all His house.
>
> Hebrews 3:1–2

The phrase *partakers of the heavenly calling* means simply this: that we hear heaven calling us. Right now heaven is calling for a people who are not living for the world, but who wake up each morning and hear Jesus calling them to Himself. They look at all that surrounds them and cry inwardly, "Jesus, my heart is not here, my future's not here. Nothing in this world satisfies me. You alone, Lord, are my life!"

I believe that many today in the Body of Christ truly are not bound to anything on this earth. You could take away their jobs, houses, bank accounts, businesses—everything but the clothes on their backs—and yet still they would love God with all their hearts. But faithfulness to God does not just mean a willingness to lose everything for His sake. In fact, Scripture says we can give our bodies to be burned at the stake as a testimony, but without the proper motive—without love in our hearts—we will die in vain (see 1 Corinthians 13:3).

Some think of faithfulness to God as simply living without lust or maintaining victory over sinful habits. Others think it means being constant in Bible reading, prayer, giving and church attendance. Still others think of it as performing good deeds, or keeping pure by avoiding all evil. These things in themselves can never make us faithful to God. You may ask, "Do you mean all my striving against sin, all my sanctified service to God and crying out in prayer are not considered faithfulness? If that's not being faithful, what is?"

All these wonderful things indeed are commanded by the Word, and we will do them if we are faithful, but in themselves they do not constitute faithfulness. Faithfulness to God is impossible unless it springs from a trusting, believing heart. Here is a very simple statement on the surface yet one we must not overlook if we are to be faithful to God: We cannot hunger for Jesus if we allow unbelief to take root in our hearts.

Unbelief in even its slightest form is hateful to God. It hinders God's work in us and it is the sin that lies behind all departure from Him. We can be totally weaned from all worldly possessions and long in our hearts for Jesus' coming. We can sit under strong preaching, sing God's praises in His house and devour the Word of God every day. But unless we're praying, "O God, let me hear Your Word in my inner man; let me believe I can apply it and that it will become life to me," then it has no effect whatsoever. The Word you hear must be mingled with faith: "The word which they heard did not profit them, not being mixed with faith in those who heard it" (Hebrews 4:2). Let those words sink in: Unless what we read and hear preached is not mixed with faith, it is of no value to us!

The verse at the opening of this chapter says that Jesus was faithful to God just as Moses was faithful. In what way was their faithfulness measured? How were Jesus and Moses truly faithful in all things? They were counted faithful *because they never doubted the heavenly Father's word to them.* They knew that what God said He would do, He would indeed do.

Faithfulness, then, is simply believing that God will keep His Word. In this sense Jesus and Moses "[held] the beginning of [their] confidence steadfast to the end" (Hebrews 3:14). They didn't have an up-and-down, here-today-and-gone-tomorrow kind of faith. Their faith never wavered to the end. And just as Jesus proved faithful in His confidence in the Father, we who make up His house will find our faithfulness measured by the same standard: "Christ [was] a Son over His own house, whose house we are if we hold fast the confidence and the rejoicing of the hope firm to the end" (Hebrews 3:6).

As our trials increase and the battle grows more intense, our flesh can become weary. Over time, many Christians allow fear and doubt to creep in, and they lose their abandonment to God, their childlike faith in Him. Caution and questioning invade their hearts. But I don't want to come to the end of my life like so many believers I have seen, whose years were wasted because they did not know where they stood in Christ. When the end came for them, I thought they would have a certain strength, that they would be refreshed to know they were nearer to meeting the Lord. Instead they went out with a whimper because they did not remain steadfast to the end. Now, as I look down the road that remains of my own life, I see limited time and I want more than anything to be rejoicing in hope, holding firm to the end.

Let me share with you how we can become faithful to God and hold fast our confidence all our days. If we want to be as strong in our last days as we are now in His presence, then we should take these two things to heart.

The Accuser

First, we must be sure never to listen to the lies of the devil.

We must remind ourselves daily that we have an enemy who is out to destroy us. He is a liar, a deceiver and seducer. Jesus said, "The devil . . . was a murderer from the beginning, and does not stand in the truth, because there is no truth in him. When he speaks a lie, he speaks from his own resources, for he is a liar and the father of it" (John 8:44).

Jesus has exposed the "father of all lies," the instigator of every deception and falsehood. He said that all lies are birthed in Satan's bosom. And God has clearly warned His Church that, especially in the last days, the devil will spend all his time accusing us: "So the great dragon was cast out, that serpent of old, called the Devil and Satan, who deceives the whole world. . . . The accuser of our brethren . . . accused them before our God day and night" (Revelation 12:9–10). The devil stands before God 24 hours a day, accusing us and spewing out lies against us. His lies are meant to disrupt our peace and confidence in God.

Satan does not waste his time lying to sinners; they are already captive, held prisoner by his deception. Instead he works on believers whose hearts are hungering for the Lord. He plants lies in the minds of the true seekers, God's holy ones. In fact, we can narrow this down even further: Satan lies to those who are determined to enter God's rest:

> There remains therefore a rest for the people of God. For he who has entered His rest has himself also ceased from his works as God did from His. Let us therefore be diligent to enter that rest, lest anyone fall according to the same example of disobedience.
>
> Hebrews 4:9–11

This "rest" means a place of total trust in God's Word. It is a place of faith where there is no struggle, fear or doubt. It is a settled rest, a continuous confidence that God is with us, that He cannot fail and that He who called us will see us through to the end.

Yet just when many of us think we are about to enter this new life of total rest and trust in the Lord, just when we think our flesh is crucified, that we no longer trust in our own works and instead depend on the Lord, then along comes the old serpent with a new pack of lies and accusations. He gets the ear of our consciences and, using horrible lies out of hell, accuses everything we do.

As I mentioned earlier, Satan's direct target is your faith in God. He knows that if your faith is allowed to grow, it will make all his lies ineffective. And when you stand before God and say, "I don't want anything in this world but Jesus," the devil knows you mean it. He knows it not just by your words but by your actions, because it is no longer merely a statement for you but a way of living. So if you really mean what you have said, then beware: All hell is going to come at you. The devil will lie to you in your prayer closet, in church and on your job. But you can rest assured that such harassment has marked the lives of all godly men and women. I have read about many dynamic people of God, and every one of them acknowledged that Satan came to them in their most productive, holy times, trying to destroy them with lies.

Here are three of the devil's biggest lies:

Lie Number One: "You are making no spiritual progress."

A voice whispers, "In spite of all your hunger for God, your self-denial and all the preaching you have absorbed, you've made no progress in your walk with Jesus. You are still sinful, hardheaded and full of self. You've been given so much, yet it has changed you so little. You wouldn't grow up spiritually even if you lived to be a hundred years old. Something is wrong with you. Others are growing and passing you by. You're just a phony, a hypocrite. You're a weak, spineless, no-good Christian!"

How many times has the devil come to you with these particular lies? First of all, Christians do not compare their growth with others'. And secondly, the devil is not the one to tell you whether or not you are growing. In fact, he would not come to you with lies unless you *were* growing.

Lie Number Two: "You are too weak for spiritual warfare."

The devil tells you, "This spiritual warfare is too much for you. You are worn out, weary and tired. You don't have the strength to go on fighting." In every waking hour he whispers, "Weary . . . worn out . . . at the end of your rope . . . give up . . . slow down . . . go easy . . . tired . . . tired . . . tired. . . . "

Daniel warned us that the devil would be successful in wearing down the saints: "He shall speak pompous words against the Most High, shall persecute the saints of the Most High" (Daniel 7:25). The Hebrew word used here is to "tire mentally, make the mind weary." Maybe you have heard that voice in your head recently: "I'm mentally drained, totally wiped out." This is not the language of the overcomer. Yes, there are times when we become physically weary or tired, but the devil wants to use those words to make us spiritually weary and to rob us of the victory and the joy that are ours in the Holy Spirit.

The fact is, much of our spiritual weariness is caused by this implanted lie from hell. Satan tells us, "Don't get so intense about the things of God, about the lost and hurting, the poor and needy. You shouldn't work so hard. Just ease off. Something is wrong— you're supposed to be at rest, but you're wearing down. You must have sin in your heart. What terrible thing is hidden in you?"

I have often heard the voice of the deceiver try to invade my study and whisper these words into my heart: "You are not a good shepherd. You have no true biblical rest in your soul. Look how hard it is for you to get a message. David, you are tired, dry. If you had faith, you would not have a daughter going through radiation and chemotherapy treatments. You would not have a cold that's hung on for weeks. You would be so full of power and revelation, multitudes would be flocking to God. You are just worn out. You have so little faith."

Where does all this come from? Straight from the pit of hell, from the father of all lies! Satan questions our faith, accuses our faith and lies about our faith.

Lie Number Three: "God is not with you. You have grieved Him away."

Satan whispers, "God still loves you. But He is not with you now. There is something in you, something unseen and unknown to you. His blessing and favor are no longer with you."

The devil will pound you with God's Word out of context. He'll say, "Didn't God leave Israel when she sinned? He cut her off and forsook her. Your present dry spell and your daily struggles are all proof that God is not with you. The Holy Spirit has left you!"

This was the lie the devil planted in Gideon's mind. Israel had been delivered into the hands of the Midianites and suffered great cruelty under them. Then God sent an angel who said to Gideon, "The Lord is with you, you mighty man of valor!" (Judges 6:12). Gideon looked around him—then heard the devil's lie and said, "If the Lord is with us, why then has all this happened to us? And where are all His miracles which our fathers told us about, saying, 'Did not the Lord bring us up from Egypt?' But now the Lord has forsaken us and delivered us into the hands of the Midianites" (Judges 6:13).

It is true that God delivered Israel to the Midianites—but only to chasten them. He never forsook His beloved people and He will never forsake His Church today. He will let us be chastened by the enemy, but when His discipline is complete, He says, "Hands off! These people are Mine."

Today we have this word: "He Himself has said, 'I will never leave you nor forsake you.' So we may boldly say: 'The Lord is my helper; I will not fear. What can man do to me?'" (Hebrews 13:5–6). "Lo, I am with you always, even to the end of the age" (Matthew 28:20). Jesus will never leave us, never forsake us. God is with us *always*.

If we have been seeking the Lord, He is with us no matter what lies we hear, no matter how we feel, no matter what our circumstances. We need to stand face to face with the devil before all the demons in hell and say, "I don't care what you say about how I feel. God is with me! If God is for me, who can be against me?" (see Romans 8:31).

The High Priest

The second word of encouragement to help us hold fast our confidence, besides never listening to the lies of the devil, is this: We must be fully persuaded that our High Priest cares and that we have full access to His throne.

> Seeing then that we have a great High Priest who has passed through the heavens, Jesus the Son of God, let us hold fast our confession. For we do not have a High Priest who cannot sympathize with our weaknesses, but was in all points tempted as we are, yet without sin. Let us therefore come boldly to the throne of grace, that we may obtain mercy and find grace to help in time of need.
>
> Hebrews 4:14–16

We have been invited into the throne room of the Potentate of the universe. And He knows what we have been through, what we are going through now and what we face ahead. "There is no creature hidden from His sight, but all things are naked and open to the eyes of Him to whom we must give account" (Hebrews 4:13). The Lord is waiting for us to come boldly to Him with everything that concerns us.

He Himself has experienced all that we are going through at all points, and He is sympathetic, loving, full of mercy and anxious to help in our time of need. Is this your time of need? Do you know He is available at any time? We don't have to say, "I've got to go home and get in my secret closet to enter God's throne room." The throne is available to us anytime and anywhere. And God invites us to come boldly and without reservation to that throne, with full confidence that He will answer, that He will always keep His Word. We don't have to explain anything to Him. We can just kneel before Him and say boldly, "Jesus, You know what I'm going through. I can't put it into words. But You've been here, too—so please help me!"

We live by promises, not by what we see. And if we are to be faithful to God, we cannot sit around nursing our doubts. Instead, we have to encourage ourselves daily in the Lord, dealing with all unbelief, saying, "Lord, I'll not put up with it!" We must reject the devil's lies and build our faith upon God's Word: "But you, beloved, building yourselves up on your most holy faith, praying in the Holy Spirit, keep yourselves in the love of God" (Jude 20–21).

～ 20 ～
THE PRESENT GREATNESS OF CHRIST

[I pray] that the God of our Lord Jesus Christ, the Father of glory, may give to you the spirit of wisdom and revelation in the knowledge of Him the eyes of your understanding being enlightened; that you may know what is the hope of His calling, what are the riches of the glory of His inheritance in the saints, and what is the exceeding greatness of His power toward us who believe, according to the working of His mighty power which He worked in Christ when He raised Him from the dead and seated Him at His right hand in the heavenly places.

Ephesians 1:17–20

In this well-known prayer, Paul wanted the Ephesian church (and the Church today) to know something important. He prayed that God would reveal to us the exceeding greatness of Christ's power—and that means not just His *past* greatness, but His *present* greatness as well.

What does this mean, the present greatness of Christ?

The Church has great reverence for the Christ who walked on

earth—the Galilean Jesus, Son of Mary, teacher and miracle-worker. We never grow tired of hearing about the greatness of Jesus of Nazareth, how He chased demons, stood strong against all temptation, opened blind eyes, unstopped deaf ears, caused paralytics to leap, restored withered limbs, healed leprosy, turned water into wine, fed multitudes with a few loaves and fishes and raised the dead.

Yet at some point in history the Church put limits on our great, mighty, miracle-working Savior. We developed a theology that made Him Lord over the spiritual but not over the natural. We believe, for example, that He can forgive our sins, calm our nerves, relieve our guilt, give us peace and joy, and offer us eternal life—all work that is done in the unseen, invisible world. But few believers know Christ as the God of the natural, of our everyday affairs—that is, the Lord over our children, jobs, bills, marriages and homes. Paul says we need a revelation of the power Christ has had *since* the time He was raised from the dead, to show us His power in all these things. Even now, he says, Jesus sits at the right hand of God, possessing all power in heaven and earth, and that God has "put *all things* under His feet" (Ephesians 1:22, emphasis mine).

As I prayed on this matter, the Holy Spirit spoke powerfully to my heart. He said, *Jesus has never been more powerful than He is right now.* Indeed, Scripture says, "[He is] far above all principality and power and might and dominion, and every name that is named, not only in this age but also in that which is to come" (Ephesians 1:21). If we really believe this, the implications for us are awesome.

He Never Gave Up on the Dead

He who conquered death has all power. And the greatest evidence of Christ's power on earth was those He raised from the dead. "For just as the Father raises the dead and gives them life, even so the Son also gives life to whom He wishes" (John 5:21, NAS). Jesus clearly claimed to have power over death. He even said of Himself, "I am the resurrection and the life" (John 11:25)—and He proved it!

But do we truly believe Jesus when He said, "The hour is coming, and now is, when the dead will hear the voice of the Son of God; and those who hear will live. For as the Father has life in Himself, so He has granted the Son to have life in Himself" (John 5:25–26)? And if so, do we realize the implications for our day-to-day lives?

As Jesus talks here of the dead rising at the sound of God's voice, He is not speaking only of the final resurrection. Jesus is also describing His present power to raise up *everything that has died*. You see, we all have a secret graveyard in our lives that holds someone or something we gave up on a long time ago. We have buried it and inscribed on its tombstone the date of its death. And whenever we think about it, we never consider the present power of Christ to give it His resurrection life.

A few years ago a dear family acquaintance told us about going to her child's graduation. Her former husband would be among the relatives who would be attending—a man who had left her years before for another woman. Our friend's marriage was beyond resurrection, since her former husband had remarried. Yet God bade our friend go back to the graduation—to the grave site of her dead marriage—and pray for the salvation of her husband and his wife. This woman did not give up on the spiritually dead.

I know another dear woman in Christ whose husband left her years ago. The man is now lost in deep sin. Where a good marriage once blossomed, a tombstone now stands. Yet she, too, has learned that Jesus never gives up on the dead. It is not that she wants her husband back (indeed, he may never come back). Rather, she wants him resurrected from the death of sin so she prays for him now. She will not give up on the dead because she knows she serves a God with present-day resurrection power.

A pastor wrote to me with this sad story: He took into his home a released convict, a man who seemed repentant. After a few months the pastor came home and found the man in bed with his wife. The man fled, but the woman had become pregnant by him. This pastor now lives in constant grief. He can barely support the two children they already have and his marriage is in a shambles. He has the added worry about AIDS from the former convict's drug use. He just can't see how he will ever make it. "It's a dead end everywhere I turn," he wrote. "It seems absolutely hopeless with no way out."

I know a father who grieves over his sixteen-year-old daughter. The girl once was innocent and loving. Now she is hooked on crack and wanders the streets to sell her body. She is physically emaciated, and she possesses the morals of an alley cat. This father loves his child dearly, but now she is half-dead—really more dead than alive. He weeps over her high school photograph, remembering the long walks and talks they enjoyed together. Now, sadly, he has given up all hope. He sits and waits for that dreaded late-night phone call telling him to come to the morgue and identify his young daughter's body.

All these victims of the devil's ravages seem to have good reason to give up on their loved ones. But Jesus never gives up on the dead! Instead, He brings life out of death. And all that anyone ever needs in any situation is His Word, His breath—and what has appeared dead and hopeless will come to life anew.

A grieving father named Jairus once came to Jesus to ask for the healing of his dying daughter:

> One of the rulers of the synagogue came, Jairus by name. And when he saw Him, he fell at His feet and begged Him earnestly, saying, "My little daughter lies at the point of death. Come and lay Your hands on her, that she may be healed, and she will live." So Jesus went with him, and a great multitude followed Him and thronged Him.
>
> Mark 5:22–24

Jairus represents most of Christianity. Like him we know Christ is our only hope and in a crisis we run to Him and fall at His feet, seeking His mercy and help. Jairus had a good measure of faith as well. He asked Jesus to come and lay His hands on the child "that she may be healed, and she will live." He was saying, "Lord, all she needs is You. You have all power. You can keep her from dying." And responding to this man's faith Jesus went with him.

Most of us in Jairus' position would undoubtedly be filled with great hope at Jesus' consent. But we might also be struck with a terrible thought: *What if we're too late? It's wonderful to have Jesus by my side but we need time. I need Jesus* and *time!* If so, we have limited faith and need a different perspective. If we call on Jesus and know who He really is—"the resurrection and the life"—we can rest in our spirits and tell our troubled hearts, "Jesus transcends time. I don't need more time—I just need Him."

The nominal believers who stood at the girl's bedside certainly had limited faith. As long as there was a little life left, they reasoned, Jesus was wanted and needed. Most likely before her death these people said to themselves, "Yes, we believe Jesus is the great Physician, the great Healer. Nothing is impossible for Him because we know He has all power. But, oh, please hurry, Lord—she may die any minute!" What kind of faith is this? It is faith only to the point of death; it believes only to the grave. And when circumstances look as if all is lost, this faith dies.

This is the faith that Mary of Bethany had. She said to Jesus after Lazarus died, "Lord, if You had been here, my brother would not have died" (John 11:32). This also was the faith Lazarus' neighbors and friends had: "Some of them said, 'Could not this Man, who opened the eyes of the blind, also have kept this man from dying?'" (11:37). Neither Mary nor Martha nor a single person at that grave site had any faith in Christ as the Resurrection. To them Jesus was powerful and much-needed—but only to the point of death.

Similarly, when the crowd around Jairus' daughter saw that she had died, they lost the little faith they had. I can see them taking her pulse and pronouncing her dead. Their first order of funeral business was to notify the Healer that He was no longer needed. So they sent a messenger to Jairus saying, "Your daughter is dead. Why trouble the Teacher any further?" (Mark 5:35).

These words must have seemed so final to Jairus: "Your daughter is dead!" I ask you, are these same words ringing in your ears? "Your marriage is dead—don't bother Jesus!" "Your ministry is dead—don't bother the Lord!" "Your child is dead in sin—don't bother Christ!" "Your relationship to that loved one is dead—give it up! Why trouble the Teacher any further?" In other words, "Why hold on when it's all over? It's a dead issue now. Leave it alone."

When the news reached Jairus of his daughter's death, he might even have said something similar: "Thanks, Lord—I know You meant well. Maybe it would have been all right if that woman with the issue of blood hadn't touched the hem of Your garment and delayed You. And I really had faith. I knew in my heart that if You arrived while my daughter was still breathing, she would live."

But no need and no person is ever too far gone for Jesus! Those dreaded words mean absolutely nothing to Him. He never gives up on the dead: He is resurrection life. In Greek, the best rendition of verse 36 is, "Jesus, as if He did not hear what was spoken, said to the ruler of the synagogue, 'Be not afraid, only believe.' "

Faith that goes only to the point of death is not good enough. Jesus allowed time to run out in this instance because He wanted His followers to have faith in His resurrection power. He wanted their faith in Him to go beyond hopelessness, beyond even death.

Jesus did not turn away, and a terrible scene occurred at Jairus' house. I am deeply saddened when I read the account of what happened when Jesus arrived there. Amid the total confusion, fear and wailing, everyone acted as if Jesus were a mourner coming to pay His last respects. I can hear them saying, "Well, at least He's decent enough to come to the funeral. Better late than never!" Mark 5:38–40 reads:

> He came to the house of the ruler of the synagogue, and saw a tumult and those who wept and wailed loudly. When He came in, He said to them, "Why make this commotion and weep? The child is not dead, but sleeping." And they ridiculed Him.

The King James Version says they "laughed him to scorn."

I ask you—is this the reason there is so much commotion in so many people's lives, so much grieving and mourning? Is it because they do not believe that Jesus can resurrect what is dead? Perhaps they don't believe Jesus knows what He is doing, that He has a life-giving plan. They think He is too late and that things have gone too far. They cannot believe Jesus is still at work on what *they* have already given up on.

As I read this account in Mark, I look at those doubting people and want to shout, "What are you laughing at? Why have you given up? Hold on, trust Him. He can raise her up! He *wants* to raise her up! It's been His plan all along."

> When He had put them all outside, He took the father and the mother of the child, and those who were with Him, and entered where the child was lying. Then He took the child by the hand, and said to her, "Talitha, cumi," which is translated, "Little girl, I say to you, arise." Immediately the girl arose and walked.
>
> Mark 5:40–42

As we hunger in our hearts for more of Jesus, He will apply His living power to our dead circumstances. We will not cry out to God in our trouble, hoping He will answer before it is too late. We will not turn into mourners when it appears that the answer has not come. We will not tremble before the power of the devil, as if he has won the victory—as if Jesus has lost and the devil has won! When things go from bad to worse we will not ever say, "That's it! It's too late, it's all over. For some reason, the Lord has chosen to let this happen. He is not going to rescue this situation."

Some may think that this final statement appears noble. But it is not enough to love, serve and worship God only to the point of hopelessness. We must trust Him when all our hope seems gone, when it looks as if we will never land a job or see our loved ones saved, when things are piling up on all sides and it appears humanly impossible to go on.

If Jesus walked into your present situation, how would He find you? And how would you react to Him? Would you still grieve? Would your heart still be in turmoil? Or would you say to Him, "Lord, it looked hopeless. I was about to give up but I know You are the same today as You were in Jairus' day! You can heal this problem. You can bring life out of death." And, when Jesus finally does work your miracle, will you be found on the outside with the scoffers or on the inside among His faithful circle? The faithful were there to see Jesus at work. And that is where we all should want to be—on the inside, the faith side!

Our faith must hold that Jesus' power goes beyond the point of death. We must look directly into the face of all that is lifeless and proclaim, "Jesus never gives up on the dead! He has never been more willing to show His power than He is right now." We can never give up on anyone or anything that Jesus desires, no matter how hopeless the situation seems.

Notice that in the story of Jairus and his daughter the Lord was not interested in showing His power to unbelievers. In fact, He commanded the ones in that room not to tell anyone about it. He said, in effect, "Don't tell them what you saw. The miracle is among us in this room." This tells us that those who hold on in unswerving faith are in for a glorious manifestation of Christ's resurrection power! Only you and the Lord will know all the intimate workings. He will astonish and thrill you—and He will show you His glory.

The present greatness of Christ can be summed up in one power-ful verse: "In Him was life" (John 1:4). Jesus was, and is now, energizing life. He was renewed constantly as He drew on a heav-enly reservoir of life. He never wearied of the crowds pressing in on Him. He was never impatient. When He called His disciples to come aside for a while to rest, they departed to a quiet place across the lake—but the crowds were waiting there, too. Not once did He say, "Oh, no! It's that problem bunch again, with their silly complaints and stupid questions. Won't it ever end?" Instead He saw the multitudes and was moved to compassion. He was energized by the Spirit and went to work. He had days of toil, nights of prayer and time for little children. In a weary moment He stopped to rest at a well, but a woman needed help. Again He was energized. His disci-ples found their Master relaxed and refreshed. "He said to them, 'I have food to eat of which you do not know' " (John 4:32). That is the secret energy of resurrection life!

Believers today have been promised the very same energizing life of Christ. And when we feel like a drained car battery we should bring this quickly to mind: "If the Spirit of Him who raised Jesus from the dead dwells in you, He who raised Christ from the dead will also give life to your mortal bodies through His Spirit who dwells in you" (Romans 8:11).

Are you full of the Holy Spirit? If so, then thank God for the present greatness of our Lord Jesus Christ. By faith draw upon His life and energy "so that your youth is renewed like the eagle's" (Psalm 103:5). And when the time comes for that final resurrection—entering into His glorious heavenly Kingdom—we will thank Him for eternity that He enabled us to walk out our earthly lives in His resurrection life and power.